Employment law for manager:
A study guide

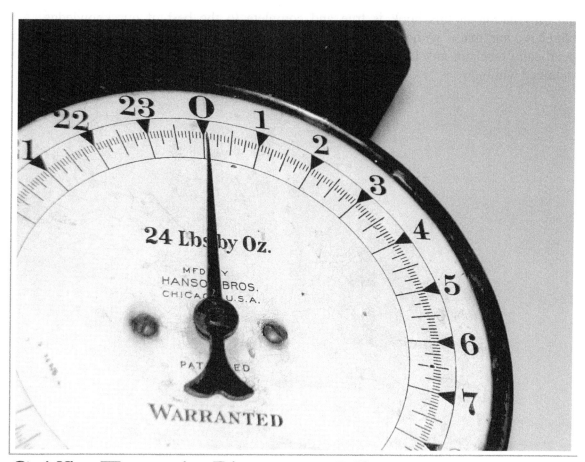

Griffin Toronjo Pivateau, J.D.
Second Edition (2013-08)

DEDICATION

This book is dedicated to the students who have helped shape its content. Many thanks.

TABLE OF CONTENTS

1. Introduction to employment law

Why study employment law?

Employment is one of the most important institutions in our lives

- It is our greatest - and perhaps only - capital asset

- Our economic and social system is based on the concept of employment

- It is where we form friendships and relationships

- Employment forms the basis for our identity

The study of employment law has additional benefits

- Employment law is a complicated mix of statutes, regulations, and case law

- Employment law is constantly changing

- The study of employment law teaches you how to think analytically

Employment law is about striking a balance

- The law tries to balance the interests of employers, employees, and society

- A decision may benefit one to the exclusion of the others

- Understanding how the balance is reached is vital for understanding employment law

Why NOT study employment law?

2. The sources of employment law

Introduction

Setting

- Understanding employment law requires understanding how the law works

- Every area of the law has sources

- There are three primary sources of employment law

- Employment law derives from constitutional law, common law, and statutory law

Objective

- In this lecture, we examine three important sources of employment law

Employment law is based in part on constitutional law

Constitutional law refers to the supreme law of the sovereign

- Constitutional law includes the fundamental law upon which the United States is based

- Constitutional law governs the creation and execution of laws by the government

- Constitutional law governs the scope of power and authority given to the government

- All government institutions, whether state or federal, must obey the United States constitution

- State constitutions are the supreme law of the state

Courts have the authority to decide whether laws passed by Congress are constitutional and therefore valid

- The United States Congress enacts laws pursuant to its powers under the Constitution

- The doctrine of judicial review gives courts the power to determine whether a law is constitutional

- The judicial system has the final say on interpreting the Constitution

Some constitutional provisions relate to employment

- The federal government's power to regulate employment is based on the commerce clause

- The privileges and immunities clause prevents states from discriminating against citizens of other states

- The first amendment to the bill of rights provides certain protections for the exercise of free speech

- The unreasonable search provision of the fourth amendment prevents some forms of search by employers

- The equal protection clause found in the fourteenth amendment may also affect employment

Employment law is based in part on the common law

What is the common law?

- The common law is also known as case law

- The common law results from judge-made decisions and interpretations

- These decisions form precedent

- The doctrine of *stare decisis* requires judges to follow precedent

Agency law provides the basis for the law of employment

- Agency law is fundamental to our legal system

- Agency is an agreement by one person to act for another at the other's direction and control

- There are always three entities involved in an agency relationship

Agents can make their principals liable to third parties

- Employees are (almost) always agents of their employer

- Agents can bind their principals for all acts within their authority

- Agents can bind their principals for negligent acts

- Employers often act only through their agents

- Not every agent of an employer, however, is an employee

Employment law is based in part on statutory law

What is statutory law?

- Statutory law is written law set down by a legislature

- A statute is an act of the legislature declaring, commanding or prohibiting something

- Statutory law reflects the will of the people speaking through their elected representatives

Statutes are a primary source of the law

- Federal statutes take precedence over state statutes, and state statutes are superior to the common law

- Statutes are subordinate to the Constitution

There are different sources of statutory law

- Federal statutes make up the U.S. Code

- Each state has its own set of statutes

- State statutes often supplement or mirror federal statutes

- Cities and counties enact municipal ordinances

- If state and federal statutes conflict, then the federal statute wins

Administrative regulations also fall within statutory law

- Statutory law is often enforced through the establishment of administrative rules

- Regulations have the effect of law as long as they lie within the limits set by the statutes

- Federal administrative regulations are gathered in the Code of Federal Regulations (CFR)

- In the employment arena, the Equal Employment Opportunity Commission (EEOC) enacts most regulations

Conclusion

- Employment law is based in part on constitutional law

- Employment law is based in part on the common law of agency

- Employment law is based in part on statutory law

3. Torts and employment law

Introduction

Setting

- Tort law is about the obligations that we owe to one another

- People rarely discuss the role of tort law in society

- Tort law defines the duties that we owe to others around us

- Tort law defines the remedies available when we fail to live live up to our duties

Objective

- In this lecture, we learn about the law of torts, how it regulates behavior, and about intentional torts

The law of torts governs the duties that we owe

People have certain interests that others have the obligation or duty to respect.

- These interests, and the duty of others to respect them, does not depend upon promises or agreements

- The violation of the duty to respect the interest is called a "tort"

- Tort law is the body of principles that defines these interests and duties

- Tort law defines the remedies available to the injured party when the duties have not been met

Tort law protects important interests

- The interest in bodily integrity.

  - Examples of the violation of this interest are:

    - Assault

    - Battery

- The interest in being free to move about.

  - The violation of this interest is false imprisonment

- The interest in one's reputation.

  - The violation of this interest is **DEFAMATION**

    - **LIBEL** (written defamation) or

    - **SLANDER** (spoken defamation)

- The interest in controlling access to one's home or place of business.

  - The violation of this interest is **TRESPASS**.

Tort law performs three roles

- Compensation of the victim

- Justice

- Prevention of future costs

The interests protected by tort law may sometimes be rightfully intruded upon

- We sometimes **CONSENT** to conduct that would otherwise be tortious

  - Consent may be **EXPRESS** or **IMPLIED**

- The doctrine of **PRIVILEGE** acknowledges that some intrusions are justified by important social goals

- **IMMUNITY** reflects the view that for certain institutions, tort principles may be inappropriate

  - Family immunity

  - Charitable immunity

  - Sovereign immunity

Many torts may arise in the employment context

Many times employers are only concerned about statutory liability

- Managers and HR professionals often focus only on statutes

  - Title VII of the 1964 Civil Rights Act

  - The Fair Labor Standards Act

  - The Family and Medical Leave Act

  - The Americans with Disabilities Act

  - The Age Discrimination in Employment Act

- Business people tend to forget common law liability

- With tort causes of action, both the employer and the employee can be liable

- In contrast, there is little risk of individual liability under employment statutes

Defamation is a common tort that occurs in employment

Defamation

- A statement is defamatory if it tends to

    1. harm the reputation of another so as to lower him in the estimation of the community; or

    2. deter third persons from associating or dealing with him; or

    3. expose him to public hatred, contempt, or ridicule.

- A statement may be false, abusive, unpleasant and objectionable to the plaintiff without being defamatory

- Expressions of opinion may be protected by the state or federal constitution

- Defamation arises most often in the employment context when the employer accused a current of former employee of inappropriate conduct

    - theft

    - illegal drug use

    - unfair competition

    - incompetence or

    - negligence

There are different types of defamation

- Libel

  1. defamation;

  2. expressed in written or graphic form;

  3. that tends to injure a person's reputation

     - Injuring a person's reputation means exposing the person to public hatred, contempt, ridicule, or financial injury, or thereby impeaching the person's honesty, integrity, virtue, or reputation.

- Slander

  1. defamation;

  2. expressed in an oral statement;

  3. that is published to a third person; and

  4. refers to an ascertainable person.

- Libel/Slander per se

  - A statement is libelous or slanderous per se if it unambiguously and falsely imputes criminal conduct to the plaintiff

There are defenses to a defamation claim

- Truth

- Consent

- Qualified privilege

There are other torts that arise in the employment context

Intentional infliction of emotional distress

- Intentional infliction of emotional distress is intentional or reckless conduct that is extreme and outrageous

- "so outrageous in character, and so extreme in degree, as to go beyond all possible bounds of decency, and to be regarded as atrocious, and utterly intolerable in a civilized community"

- Courts have limited the use of intentional infliction of emotional distress in employment law

- Usually available only when the plaintiff can show facts **independent** of a parallel statutory claim.

- Advice: be careful of the "screamer"

Assault and battery

- a plaintiff must prove that the defendant:

  - Intentionally caused an apprehension of an offensive touching

  - Intentionally caused an offensive touching

- Advice: no unnecessary touching of employees

False imprisonment

- Usually occurs when the employee is detained for some reason

- elements of a false imprisonment cause of action are:

  1. a willful detention;

2. without consent; and

3. without authority of law.

- A detention may be accomplished by violence, threats, or by any other means that restrains a person from moving from one place to another.

- Advice: Don't block your employees from the exit

Fraud

- Elements

  1. Misrepresentation of material fact (Including failure to disclose – "duty to disclose")

  2. Knowledge of its falsity or reckless disregard for truth

  3. Intent to deceive (induce reliance), and where

  4. plaintiff takes action in justifiable reliance

  5. Causing economic damages

- Silence is not usually enough

- Advice: don't make promises that you don't intend to keep

Invasion of privacy

- Invasion of privacy occurs when a person "unreasonably and seriously interferes with another's interest in not having his affairs known to others."

- Right to monitor may end when you have the information you need

- Advice: limit privacy invasions to legitimate needs of the company

Intentional interference with valid contractual relations

- Elements

    1. Valid contract or economic expectancy

    2. Defendant has knowledge (knew or should of known – knowledge of the facts which form a contract, not necessarily that those facts actually form a contract) of the valid contract or economic expectancy, and

    3. The defendant intends to interfere (Intent = Purposeful interference and knowledge with substantial certainty that interference will occur)

    4. The defendant causes interference, and

    5. Plaintiff suffers damage

There may be justifications for interference with economic expectation or contractual relations:

- Stating truthful information or honest advice within the scope of a request

- Acting to protect the welfare of another when charged to protect that welfare

- The contract is illegal or against public policy

- Protecting bona fide interests through good faith and means

- In the employment context, this tort often arises in connection with noncompete agreements

- Advice: carefully interview prospective employees about their pre-existing commitments

Conclusion

- The law of torts governs the duties that we owe to others around us

- Defamation is a common tort that occurs in employment

- There are other torts that arise in the employment context

4. Ethics and the business manager

Introduction

Setting

- Ethical challenges face managers daily

- Managers have the potential to change, shape, redirect, and alter the course of other people's lives

- Managers make decisions that reward some with salaries, benefits, knowledge, and skills

- Managers will also engage in acts that harm people

Objective

- In this lecture, we study the consequences that a business manager's ethical decisions will have for individuals, organizations, and society

What is ethics?

Ethics is the study of right and wrong behavior

- Ethics consist of moral principles and values applied to social behavior

- Ethical criteria can determine whether an action is fair, right or just

- In business, ethical decisions are the application of moral and ethical principles to the marketplace and workplace

There are different approaches to ethical reasoning

Ethical reasoning is the process by which an individual examines a situation according to his or her ethical standards

- Ethical reasoning aids in making morally ambiguous decisions

There are different ethical reasoning approaches

- Duty-based ethics

- Outcome-based ethics

- Corporate social responsibility

Duty-Based Ethics: Ethics based upon an underlying concept of duty regardless of the consequences

Religious ethical standards

- Duty based ethics can arise from religious belief

- Religious standards provide that when an act is prohibited by religious teachings, it is unethical and should not be undertaken

- The consequences of the act are immaterial to the ethical decision

Kantian ethics

- Immanuel Kant believed that people should be respected because they are qualitatively different from other physical objects

- Kant was not religious in the sense that we think of it

- Kant's categorical imperative states that individuals should evaluate their actions in light of what would happen if everyone acted the same way

The Principle of Rights

- Some hold to the principle that persons have rights (to life and liberty, for example)

- In deciding whether an action is ethical, one should consider what effect her actions would have on the fundamental rights of others

- A key factor in determining whether a business decision is ethical is how that decision affects the rights of others, including employees, customers, and society.

- One must determine which rights take priority

Outcome-Based Ethics: Ethics based upon the consequences of action taken or foresworn, without regard to any underlying concept of duty or morality

Outcome-based ethics are often known as utilitarianism

- Utilitarianism focuses on the consequences of an action, not the nature of it

- An action is morally correct where it produces the greatest amount of good for the greatest number of people

- A decision to act or not act should be directed to producing the greatest good for the greatest number of people.

Businesses often employ the utilitarian approach to decision making

- Applying utilitarianism requires:

    1.1. a determination of who will be affected;

    1.2. a cost-benefit analysis—an assessment of the negative and positive effects of alternatives on those affected;

    1.3. a choice among alternatives that will produce maximum societal utility (the greatest positive benefits for the greatest number of individuals).

Corporate social responsibility

The question of corporate social responsibility concerns the extent to which a corporation should act ethically and be accountable to society in that regard

- The Stakeholder Approach

    - Stakeholders include employees, customers, creditors, suppliers, and the community within which a business operates. It is sometimes said that duties to these groups should be weighed against the duty to a firm's owners.

- The Corporate Citizenship Approach

    - Corporations are sometimes urged to actively promote social goals.

    - Some companies publish annual corporate social responsibility—or sustainability, or citizenship—reports to highlight their activities.

Making ethical decisions

Areas to consider in making ethical decisions

- The law: Is the action you are considering legal?

- Business rules and procedures: Is the action you are considering consistent with company policies and procedures?

- Social values: Is your proposed action consistent with the "spirit" of the law, even if it is not specifically prohibited?

- Your conscience: How does your conscience regard your plan? Could your plan survive the glare of publicity?

- Promises to others: Will your action satisfy your commitments to others, inside and outside the firm?

- Heroes: How would your hero regard your action?

Applying ethical standards to employment decisions

Creating ethical standards for governing employment practices

- The business manager needs ethical standards for governing employment practices

- In creating the standard, the manager must decide whose interest it protects

- The manager must then analyze the problems arising out of enforcement of the standard

In any employment action, the manager should:

- Advance the organization's objective

- Recognize the issues created by executing morally ambiguous tasks

- Enhance the dignity of those harmed by the action

Advance the organization's objective

- Employment decisions should advance the central objective of the organization

- This standard requires managers to identify the objective that their actions are supposed to serve

- This standard provides a clear and consistent direction

Recognizing the issues created by executing morally ambiguous tasks

- Recognize the positive and negative consequences of an employment decision

- Recognize the moral sensibility of those required to carry out tasks

- Attend to the experience of those carrying out decisions

Enhance the dignity of those harmed by the action

- Ensure fundamental respect for employees by treating people with fair procedures

- Treat people in a consistent and equitable manner

- Preserve and restore the ability of the harmed individual to act effectively

Conclusion

- Ethics is the study of right and wrong behavior

- There are different approaches to ethical reasoning

- The business manager needs ethical standards for governing employment practices

5. Litigation of employment disputes

Introduction

Setting

- Disputes often arise between the employer and its employees

- Disputes between employer and employees are often settled in court

- Resolving disputes in court is called litigation

- It is important to understand the court system to mange employees

Objective

- In this lecture, we look at forms of dispute resolution used in employment law

Employment disputes may be resolved in state or federal court

The court system includes multiple levels of courts

- Trial courts decide the facts of each case

- Intermediate appeals courts focus on questions of law and not fact

- The decisions of a state's highest court on state law issues are final

The federal court system has three levels

- Every state has at least one U.S. District Court

- U.S. Courts of Appeal hear appeals from trial courts within their district

- The United States Supreme Court is the highest federal court

Similar procedural rules apply in state and federal court

- Every new lawsuit goes through certain stages

- Pleadings are the documents that set out each party's claims and defenses

- The plaintiff files a Complaint to start the lawsuit

- The defendant responds to the suit in an Answer

- The defendant admits or denies the allegations

- At trial, the jury will decide the facts

Appellate courts decide questions of law

How to distinguish a fact issue from a legal issue?

- A jury is required to decide what events actually occurred

- The appellate court is required to determine what rules to apply to the facts

- An appellate court must accept the facts as determined by the trial court

The appellate court follows its own rules of procedure

- Either party can ask the appellate court to review the case

- Each side argues its case to the court of appeals

- After having decided the case, the court will issue an opinion

- The losing party may ask the Supreme Court to review the case, but it is not obligated to do so

How to read a case

- Legal cases are identified by a "legal citation" (or a "cite") as in the sample below:

    - Morse v. Frederick, 127 S.Ct. 2618 (U.S. 2007).

- Every case contains the name of the judge who authored the opinion

- Every case contains a description of the facts and a statement of the applicable law

- Every case will draw a conclusion based on application of the law to the facts

The litigation of employment discrimination litigation differs from normal lawsuits

The law requires that a discrimination plaintiff go through an administrative procedure before filing a lawsuit

- An employment plaintiff must file a charge of discrimination with an appropriate agency before filing suit

- The Equal Employment Opportunity Commission is the federal agency that administers many federal employment statutes

- The EEOC oversees the enforcement of the following federal employment statutes

    - Title VII of the Civil Rights Act

    - The Americans with Disabilities Act

- The Age Discrimination in Employment Act
- An employee with a cause of action under these statutes must file a charge with the EEOC before filing suit

The employee must meet the statute of limitations

- An employment plaintiff has 180 days to file a charge with the EEOC
- States have their own statutes protecting against discrimination in employment
- Most states have an agency that acts in the same manner as the EEOC

A state agency is called a fair employment practices agency (FEPA)

- An employee may file his claim (called a **charge**) with either the state FEPA or the EEOC
- The charge must include specific information
- Each agency has a prescribed charge-handling process
- The agency will usually immediately refer the case to mediation
- The agency then investigates the claim

The agency may do one of two things

- The agency may litigate the suit in federal court
- The agency may issue a notice of right to sue

Conclusion

- Employment disputes may be resolved in state or federal court
- Appellate courts decide questions of law

- The litigation of employment discrimination litigation differs from normal lawsuits

6. Alternate means of dispute resolution

Introduction

Setting

- Increasingly, disputes are decided outside of the court system

- There are different forms of alternate dispute resolution

- Alternate dispute resolution is growing more important in employment litigation

- Recent Supreme Court decisions indicate that most employment disputes will be consigned to private processes

Objective

- In this lecture, we examine alternate forms of employment dispute resolution

Increasingly, disputes are decided outside of the court system

Alternate dispute resolution entered the employment arena through collective bargaining

- Until the 1970s, employment disputes were generally resolved in court

- Arbitration and mediation were often parts of collective bargaining agreements

- In the 1990s, more and more disputes were shifted into private processes

- Courts are willing to apply contract principles

- Case discussion: <u>Rent-A-Center, West v. Jackson</u>, 130 S.Ct. 2772 (2010)

There are different forms of alternate dispute resolution

- Mediation is an informal nonbinding procedure

- Arbitration, a formal procedure, binds both parties to the result

- The parties may agree to a summary trial

- Judges may hold a judicial settlement conference

Arbitration is a formal means of alternate dispute resolution

Arbitration has been used more often in recent years

- Arbitration was once used primarily in collective bargaining situations

- The enforceability of the arbitration agreement is often litigated

- In this lecture, employment agreements often include an arbitration clause

- The scope of authority given to the arbitrator is often an issue

Arbitration is governed by statutes

- The Federal Arbitration Act governs most arbitrations

- Each state generally has an applicable arbitration act

Arbitration resembles a court case

- The arbitration proceeding is adversarial

- At an arbitration, the parties present evidence and witnesses

- The rules of evidence don't usually apply

Parties end up in arbitration in different ways

- The contract at issue may contain an agreement to arbitrate

- The parties may agree to arbitration at the time of dispute

- A court may order the parties to arbitration

Arbitration is generally a binding procedure

- The arbitration is conducted in front of a neutral third party or parties

- There is generally no appeal of an arbitration award

- Case discussion: Hall Street Associates, LLC v. Mattel, Inc., 128 S.Ct. 1396 (2008)

Mediation uses a neutral third party to resolve disputes in an informal procedure

Mediation is designed to facilitate an early resolution of the dispute

- Generally all disputes are now subject to mediation

- The agreement at dispute may provide for mediation

- Courts will always order a dispute to mediation before trial

Mediation contains several advantages

- Mediation is a private, confidential, and inexpensive process

- In a mediation, the parties control their fate

- A mediation agreement may be enforced in a court

Mediation has disadvantages

- Mediation relies on each party having a good faith desire to settle the case

- Mediation does not provide an independent means for the discovery of evidence

- Enforcement of a mediation agreement requires court intervention

- Private resolution of disputes prevents the growth of the common law

Conclusion

- Employment disputes are increasingly resolved in private processes

- Arbitration is a formal means of alternate dispute resolution

- Mediation uses a neutral third party to resolve disputes in an informal procedure

7. Defining the employment relationship

Introduction

Setting

- The employment relationship has experienced numerous changes

- The employment relationship has become subject to greater government regulation

- The struggle between freedom of contract and regulation of employment produces conflict

- The question of employee status makes the regulation of employment more difficult

Objective

- In this lecture, we examine the evolving nature of the employment relationship

An employer can make employment decisions that are not based on wrongful grounds

The institution of employment is a fairly recent innovation

- Historically, laborers and owners had a relationship beyond mere employment

- These historic rules evolved into the master-servant relationship

- Under the common law, the master had a duty to give legal orders and to treat his servant well

- The servant had a duty to obey all legal orders

- The master servant relationship led to the concept of *respondeat superior*

The employment at will doctrine underlies employment law in the United States

- The at will doctrine has its roots in the Industrial Revolution

- Case discussion: <u>Crews v. Buckman Laboratories, International</u>, 78 S.W. 3d 852 (Tenn. 2002)

- Any hiring is presumed to be at will

- The employer is free to discharge individuals for good cause, or bad cause, or no cause at all

- The employee is equally free to quit, strike, or otherwise cease work

The law presumes that employees are hired as at will employees

- Employees do not generally have any due process rights

- In recent years the employment at will doctrine eroded

- The at will doctrine is regulated by state, and not federal, policy

- States differ in the application of the employment at will doctrine

- Montana has legislatively ended the doctrine

- Arizona has enacted a law embracing the at will doctrine

The Industrial Revolution created the modern institution of employment

- The regulation of employment often requires a balancing act

- The Industrial Revolution also brought about the need for regulation

- Many people disagree about the nature and extent of employment regulation

- Government has taken a more active role in the regulation of employment

- Employers need to understand regulation

The question of employee status is critical to understanding regulation

Who is an employee and who is an independent contractor?

- It does not matter what the employer and the worker call themselves

- Courts, employers, and the government generally agree on the definition of employer

- An employer is one who uses others to do his work, or to work on his behalf

Courts, employers, and regulators cannot agree on the definitions of employee

- The word employee is used throughout the law but the definition is not consistent

- Under Title VII, the term employee means an individual employed by an employer

- The National Labor Relations Act defines employee as an individual who is not an independent contractor

- Workers would usually, but not always, prefer to be classified as employees

- Employers would usually, but not always, prefer workers to be classified as independent contractors

Incorrect classification of employee status can have severe consequences

- Incorrect classification may make the employer liable for violations of state and federal statutes

    - Employer payroll deductions

    - Benefits

    - Discrimination claims

    - Liability concerns

- The costs of a classification mistake can be high

- The Internal Revenue Service (IRS) can impose large fines

- The employer may be liable for violations of the National Labor Relations Act (NLRA)

- The employer may also be liable under the Fair Labor Standards Act (FLSA)

- The employer may be vicariously liable for the acts of the worker

A number of factors are used to determine whether an individual is an employee

- It usually does not matter what the parties call themselves

- Case discussion: Vizcaino v. Microsoft, 97 F. 3d 1187 (9th Cir. 1996)

- Article: Defining employee status

Employee status is ultimately decided based on the facts of the case

- There are three main tests for employee status

    - The common law agency test

    - The IRS 20-factor analysis

    - The economic realities test

The common law agency test focuses on right of control

- Historically, the most important factor in employee status analysis was "right of control"

- The common law test dates from the master-servant rule and the law of agency

- The employer need not control the work – he only has to have the right to control the work

- The common law test is commonly used in determining income tax and FICA withholding issues

- Case discussion: Estrada v Fedex Ground Package System, Inc, 154 Cal. App. 4th 1 (2d Dist. 2007)

The IRS uses a multi factor analysis to decide whether a worker is an employee

- The IRS uses three main characteristics to determine the relationship between businesses and workers:

  - Behavioral Control

  - Financial Control

  - Type of Relationship

- A decision by the IRS as to employee status has huge financial ramifications

- The parties can submit a questions in advance to the IRS as to how parties are related

- Case Discussion: <u>NLRB v Friendly Cab Co.</u>, 512 F. 3d 1090 (9th Cir. 2008)

The economic reality test exams the actual relationship between the parties

- The economic reality test looks at the following factors:

  - Right to control performance

  - Meaningful opportunity for profit or loss

  - Investment in equipment/material

  - Special skills

  - Permanency of relationship

  - Integral part of business

- Case Discussion: <u>Brock v Mr. W Fireworks, Inc.</u>, 814 F. 2d 1042 (5th Cir. 1987)

- A recent case has stressed the entrepreneurial aspect of the relationship

- Case Discussion: <u>FedEx Home Delivery v NLRB</u>, 563 F. 3d 492 (DC Cir. 2009)

What to do about contingent or temporary workers?

The permatemp has become much more common in society

- A contingent worker is one whose job is temporary, sporadic, or differs in any way from the norm of full-time employment

- The temporary work force makes up 26% of American workers

- What can temporary workers look forward to?

  - No health insurance

  - No sick days

  - No paid vacation

  - No retirement plan

  - No severance pay

  - Higher rates of depression and anxiety

Contingent workers could be entitled to some protection under employment laws

- Temporary workers may be excluded from corporate culture

- Temporary workers can be hired directly or through a staffing agency

- An employer may have several reasons why it hires through a staffing agency

- In the case of staffing firms, a worker may have TWO employers simultaneously

- Courts will examine a number of factors to determine which employer may be primarily liable

Conclusion

- An employer can make any employment decision, as long as it is not based on wrongful grounds

- The issues of employee and employer status are critical for regulation

- The next decade will see the hiring of more temporary workers

8. Proving discrimination: an overview of Title VII

Introduction

Setting

- The employment at will doctrine does not apply to cases of illegal discrimination

- Title VII of the Civil Rights Act of 1964 governs illegal discrimination in employment

- Despite laws against discrimination, employment litigation continues to grow

- Understanding Title VII is vital for all managers

Objective

- In this lecture, we look at what Title VII is, what it does, and how to prove an illegal discrimination case.

What does Title VII do?

Title VII protects against employment discrimination on the basis of membership in protected classes

- Title VII protects five classes

- Title VII protects individuals against employment discrimination on the bases of race and color

- Title VII protects individuals against employment discrimination on the bases of national origin, sex, and religion

What does Title VII say?

- It shall be an unlawful employment practice for an employer -
  to fail or refuse to hire or to discharge any individual, or
  otherwise to discriminate against any individual ... because
  of such individual's race, color, religion, sex, or national
  origin ...

Title VII's protections include the following

- Employment requirements must be uniformly and consistently applied

- Title VII prohibits offensive conduct that alters the conditions of employment

- Title VII prohibits discrimination in compensation

- Title VII prohibits physical segregation based on protected class

- Title VII protects employees who make a complaint from retaliation

Title VII does not apply to every employer

- An employer must have more than 15 employees

- Some institutions may be exempt

- Case discussion: <u>Petruska v. Gannon University</u>, 350 F. Supp. 2d 666 (W. D. PA 2004)

- Independent contractors are exempt

What was the reason for Title VII?

Title VII has its roots in the Fourteenth Amendment

- The amendment included a broad definition of citizenship

- The amendment guaranteed citizens the equal protection of the laws

- The amendment applied the Bill of Rights to the states

After the Civil War, Congress attempted to restructure the United States

- The Thirteenth Amendment prohibited slavery

- The Fourteenth Amendment guaranteed equal protection of the laws

- The Fifteenth Amendment attempted to protect political freedom

- The Civil Rights Act of 1866 attempted to protect social freedom

- Few provisions were made to protect economic freedom

Title VII permits an employee to sue in court for illegal discrimination

There are two different theories on which an employee can base his claim of illegal discrimination

- Disparate treatment involves a policy or action that is discriminatory on its face

- Disparate impact involves policies that are neutral on their face, but which have a negative impact on a protected class

- Proving a claim under Title VII is a burden-shifting process

Disparate treatment is used for cases of discrimination against an individual rather than a group

- The employee must prove a prima facie case

- The prima facie case gives rise to a presumption of unlawful discrimination

- There are four elements to a prima facie case

  - Plaintiff belongs to a protected class

  - Plaintiff applied for and was qualified for the job

  - Plaintiff was rejected

  - The position remained open and the employer sought applicants with comparable skills

- The employer rebuts the prima facie case by showing a legitimate, non-discriminatory reason (LNDR)

- The plaintiff can prove the LNDR is actually a pretext to hide unlawful discrimination

An employer may establish a Bona Fide Occupational Qualification (BFOQ) defense for certain disparate treatment cases

- BFOQ is available only for disparate treatment cases involving gender, religion and national origin

- A BFOQ is legalized discrimination

- The employer must show that this preference goes to the essence of its business

- Case discussion: <u>Wilson v. Southwest Airlines Company</u>, 517 F. Supp 292 (ND Tex 1981)

Disparate impact exists where an employer has a policy that is neutral on its face but has a negative impact upon a protected category

- Disparate impact relates to groups of employees and not individuals

- Disparate impact regulates the use of screening devices

- Case discussion: <u>Griggs v. Duke Power Co.</u>, 401 U.S. 424 (1971)

There are several methods for establishing a prima facie case of disparate impact

- The plaintiff must prove his prima facie case (generally using statistics)

- The plaintiff can show that the protected employees do not fare at least 80% as well as the majority under the policy

- Nonscored objective criteria can also create disparate impact

- Subjective criteria may be subject to disparate impact analysis too

After the plaintiff makes a prima facie case, the burden shifts to the employer

- The employer rebuts by attacking the plaintiff's statistics

- The employer can also rebut by establishing that the screening device is a business necessity

- The plaintiff can rebut by proving that there is a less discriminatory alternative

Title VII provides remedies for violation of the statute

Historically, Title VII provided only equitable remedies

- The statute provides for equitable remedies:

  - Back pay, for up to two years

  - Front pay, if reinstatement is not possible

  - Reinstatement, if feasible

  - Retroactive seniority

  - Injunctive relief

  - Attorney fees

- The Civil Rights Act of 1991 provided the recovery of compensatory damages and punitive damages

- Punitive damages are not recoverable in a disparate impact case

- The Civil Rights Act of 1991 also added the right to a jury trial

Conclusion

- Title VII protects against employment discrimination

- Disparate treatment is used for cases of discrimination against an individual rather than a group

- Disparate impact focuses on the negative impact of policies which are neutral on their face

- Title VII provides equitable and legal remedies

9. The hiring process

Introduction

Setting

- Legal issues often arise during the hiring process

- The hiring process is composed of recruitment, information gathering, and testing before employment

- The business manager who neglects this area may expose his company to liability

Objective

- In this lecture, we study the legal implications of three aspects of the hiring process

Employers may stumble over legal issues in recruitment

Recruitment is regulated by both statutes and common law

- The law gives employers leeway in connection with their recruitment practices

- Employers may discriminate, as long as it is not based on membership in one of the protected classes

Federal and state statutes govern the recruitment process

- What federal statutes govern recruitment?

  - Title VII of the Civil Rights Act of 1964

  - Americans with Disabilities Act

  - Age Discrimination in Employment Act

  - Immigration Reform and Control Act of 1986

The common law regulates recruitment through the law of misrepresentation and fraud

- Employers may become legally responsible to employees for false statements

- These situations often involve comments made about job terms or the company's current financial condition

- Misrepresentations could also involve statements about the employee's continuing job security, promotions, or benefits

- The misrepresentation need not actually be a false statement--a false impression may be enough

- An employer's silence may constitute misrepresentation

- Fraud in recruitment occurs when misstatements are used to discourage potential applicants from pursuing positions

Common recruitment techniques could lead to a claim of employment discrimination

- Advertisements

- Word-of-mouth recruiting

- Nepotism

- Promoting from within

- Venue recruiting

- Walk-in applicants

- Neutral solicitation

- There are concerns with the collection of resumes

Information gathering and selection are also potential trouble areas

During the application process, information is gathered that is designed to screen out applicants

- Appropriate questions are business-related and used for a nondiscriminatory purpose

- Only a few questions are strictly prohibited

- Some questions are not prohibited but are dangerous

- Even use of a common employment application can result in potential liability

An employer may be liable for negligent hiring

- An employer should verify the qualifications of the applicant

- Try to insure that there is no undiscovered information

- An employer must exercise reasonable care in hiring applicants who may pose a risk to others

There may be potential liability for providing references

- In recent years, many employers have grown wary of the risk involved in responding to reference inquiries

- Employers may be liable for defamation

- Employers may be liable for negligent misrepresentation

- Some states have provided immunity for reference responses

- There is no immunity for an employer who gives a negative reference in retaliation for a Title VII claim

Testing is the third part of the hiring process

Pre-employment testing carries risk

- Pre-employment testing has become standard in the selection process

- Does the test accurately test for the characteristics sought?

Testing in the work place has taken two forms

- Testing for eligibility

- Tests for ineligibility

Legality of eligibility testing

- There are Title VII implications to testing

- Certain tests may have a disparate impact upon members of a protected class

- When do decisions based on disparate impact become disparate treatment?

- Case discussion: Ricci v. DeStefano, 129 S. Ct. 2658 (2009)

- Case note: Ricci v. DeStefano

If a test has been professionally developed and validated, Title VII does not prohibit its use

- An employer must establish that the test is a business necessity, as well as predictive of job performance

- Even where these two requirements have been satisfied, the test may be challenged if a less discriminatory alternative exists

There are other forms of eligibility testing

- Integrity and personality testing have become more predominant

- Physical ability tests may be administered to applicants

- Many employers require pre-employment, post-offer medical tests

Testing for ineligibility may cause problems

- Why would an employer want to test for ineligibility?

  - The employer may wish to reduce workplace injury

  - An employer may use to tests in order to predict employee performance

  - Testing can reduce the employer's financial responsibility to the workers' compensation system

Under most circumstances, employers may test applicants

- Private testing does not generally raise constitutional implications

- State statutes may establish private sector requirements for workplace testing

- Private sector testing may result in common law invasion of privacy

- Workers may claim reckless or negligent infliction of emotional distress

- An employee may have a claim for defamation

There are other problems with ineligibility testing

- Polygraphs are notoriously unreliable (and possibly illegal)

- Drug and alcohol tests are routinely given

- Case discussion: National Treasury Employees Union v. Von Raab, 489 U.S. 656 (1989)

- Genetic testing is the next area to watch

Conclusion

- Recruitment of employees is regulated by both statutes and the common law

- There are multiple legal issues related to information gathering and selection

- Testing is the third part of the hiring process

10. Race and color discrimination

Introduction

Setting

- The drafters of the Civil Rights Act of 1964 were most concerned with racial discrimination

- No adequate definition of race exists

- The concept of race is a recent invention

- Despite years of effort, the problems of racial discrimination remain

Objective

- In this lecture,, we look at Title VII's treatment of racial discrimination

Title VII was aimed at racial discrimination

Title VII makes racial discrimination illegal

- It shall be an unlawful employment practice for an employer—
  - (1) to fail or refuse to hire or to discharge any individual, or otherwise to discriminate against any individual with respect to his compensation, terms, conditions, or privileges of employment, because of such individual's race, color …

A background to Title VII

- History and its effects account for much of today's race discrimination

- Slavery lasted for over 200 years as an integral part of American life

- A number of legal structures institutionalized race

The Reconstruction era Civil Rights Act discouraged racial discrimination

- The 1866 Civil Rights Act included three sections related to employment

- The Reconstruction Era acts remain relevant today.

- Actions under the Reconstruction Era acts must be brought by the employee suing the employer in court

42 U.S.C. Section 1981 is arguably the most important section

- §1981 guarantees equal rights under the law to make and enforce contracts

- Case discussion: <u>Patterson v. McLean Credit Union</u>, 491 U.S. 164 (1989)

- The Civil Rights Act of 1991 overturned the Patterson decision

42 U.S.C. Section 1983 protects against discrimination involving state action

- §1983 protects citizens for deprivation of their Constitutional rights under color of state law

- Section 1983 applies to public employers and to those associated with a governmental entity

- Case discussion: <u>Jett v. Dallas Independent School District</u>, 491 U.S. 701 (1989)

42 U.S.C. Section 1985 is aimed at conspiracies

- §1985 prohibits a conspiracy to interfere with Civil Rights

- §1985 addresses conspiracies to interfere with or deprive the civil rights of others

- Case discussion: <u>Mississippi Burning</u>

Title VII covers two areas: racial discrimination and racial harassment

The notion of race has expanded

- The EEOC uses different factors to determine race

- EEOC guidelines to determine race

  - Ancestry

  - Physical characteristics

  - Race-linked illness

  - Culture

  - Perception

  - Association

- Case discussion: <u>Alonzo v. Chase Manhattan Bank, NA</u>, 25 F. Supp. 2d 455 (S.D.N.Y. 1998)

Title VII prohibits discrimination on the basis of race

- Title VII places obligations on employers

- The employer must ensure that every employee has an equal opportunity

- Employers must be vigilant to guard against overt and subtle manifestations of race discrimination

A case of racial discrimination may be established by disparate treatment or disparate impact

- Disparate treatment may be shown by direct or indirect evidence of discrimination

- Disparate impact may be more difficult to discern

- Race cannot be used as a bona fide occupational qualification.

A word about color

- Case discussion: <u>Walker v. Secretary of the Treasury, Internal Revenue Service</u>, 742 F. Supp. 670 (N.D. Ga. 1990)

- Recognizing race discrimination may be an issue

- The latest EEOC statistics indicate that race remains the most frequent type of claim filed with the agency.

There are other issues related to racial discrimination

An employer may be liable for racial harassment

- To hold an employer liable for racial harassment, the employee must show that the harassment was:

  - Unwelcome

- Based on race

- So severe or pervasive that it altered the conditions of employment and created an abusive environment

Proper management strategies can avoid race claims

- Keep certain general considerations in mind

- Race discrimination may occur against any group and is equally prohibited under Title VII

- Believe that race discrimination occurs and be wiling to acknowledge it when it is alleged

- Make sure there is a top-down message that the workplace will not tolerate race discrimination in any form

- Don't shy away from discussing race when the issues arises.

- Provide a positive, non-threatening, constructive forum for the discussion of racial issues.

- When an employee reports race discrimination, don't tell the employee he or she must be mistaken.

- Be willing to treat the matter as a misunderstanding if it is clear that is what has taken place

- Offer training in racial awareness and sensitivity.

- Constantly monitor workplace hiring, termination, training, promotion, raises, and discipline to ensure that they are fair and even-handed

Conclusion

- Title VII was aimed primarily at racial discrimination

- Title VII covers two areas: racial discrimination and racial harassment

- Proper management strategies can avoid claims

11. Sex discrimination

Introduction

Setting

- Sex discrimination differs from race discrimination

- Protection against discrimination on the basis of sex was a last-minute addition to Title VII

- Courts have struggled with balancing societal interests

- Gender-related claims continue to increase

Objective

- In this lecture, we study the basics of sex discrimination

Title VII prohibits discrimination in employment based on sex

Sex-based differences in the workplace continue

- The law prohibits discrimination on the basis of sex in employment practices

- Case discussion: <u>Wedow v. City of Kansas City, Missouri</u>, 442 F. 3d 661 (8th Cir. 2006)

- Sometimes policies may not appear illegal or be intended for illegal purposes, but ...

- Case discussion: <u>Dothard v. Rawlinson</u>, 433 U.S. 321 (1977)

Employers may only select employees based on their sex if a particular gender is a bona fide occupational qualification (BFOQ)

- Gender may be used as a bona fide occupational qualification under certain limited circumstances

- Attempts to use a gender based BFOQ rarely succeed

- Case discussion: <u>Diaz v. Pan American</u>, 311 F.Supp. 559 (S.D. FL 1970)

A BFOQ may only be justified by business necessity and not business convenience

- BFOQs may be supported by community standards of morality or propriety

- Sex stereotyping is another form of gender discrimination

- Employers may not make employment decisions on the basis of stereotypes

- Case discussion: <u>Price Waterhouse v. Hopkins</u>, 490 U.S. 228 (1989)

- The mixed-motive problem: An illegal factor cannot be considered in making an employment decision

Sex discrimination may appear in different ways

Gender-plus discrimination is a form of sex discrimination

- Gender-plus discrimination involves the placing of additional requirements on employees of a certain sex

- Employers may hire women in general but not hire women with certain other factors

- Case discussion: <u>Phillips v. Martin Marietta Corp.</u>, 400 U.S. 542 (1971)

Grooming codes raise issues of sex discrimination

- Workplace grooming codes may relate to sex stereotyping

- Courts give employers a great deal of leeway to determine workplace dress code

- Case discussion: <u>Harper v. Blockbuster Entertainment Corporation</u>, 139 F. 3d 1385 (11th Cir. 1998)

- Not every difference in dress codes based upon gender is illegal

- Case discussion: <u>Jespersen v. Harrah's Operating Co.</u>, 444 F. 3d 1104 (9th Cir. 2006)

Customer or employee preferences raise issues of sex discrimination

- Title VII does not permit the employer to consider customer or employee preferences

- The Civil Rights Act of 1991 extended Title VII to U.S. citizens employed by American companies outside the United States

The Equal Pay Act prohibits pay differentials based on sex

Equal work under the EPA need only be substantially equivalent

- Equal effort involves substantially equivalent physical or mental exertion needed for performance of the jobs

- Equal skills includes substantially equivalent experience, training, education, and ability

- Equal responsibility includes a substantially equivalent degree of accountability

- Working conditions include the physical surroundings and hazards involved in a job

There are defenses to liability under the Equal Pay Act

- Pay differentials could result from

  - seniority system

  - merit pay system

  - productivity-pay system

  - or a "factor other than sex"

- Seniority systems must be bona fide and apply equally to all employees

- Merit pay systems must consist of a formal system using objective determination of employees' merit

- The factor other than sex is a broad defense

- Case discussion: Laffey v. Northwest Airlines, 567 F. 2d 429 (1976)

The EEOC enforces the Equal Pay Act

- A party may sue under the Equal Pay Act separately

- Remedies under the EPA include back pay and an equal amount as liquidated damages

- Case discussion: <u>Ledbetter v. Goodyear Tire & Rubber Co.</u>, 550 U.S. 618 (2007)

- The Lilly Ledbetter Fair Pay Act of 2009 changed the statute of limitations for equal pay claims

Conclusion

- Title VII prohibits discrimination in employment based on sex

- Gender discrimination may appear in different ways

- The Equal Pay Act prohibits sex-based pay differentials between men and women performing substantially equivalent work

12. Sexual harassment

Introduction

Setting

- Sexual harassment has received a good deal of attention since the 1990s

- Sexual harassment costs employers millions of dollars

- Sexual harassment constitutes a form of sex discrimination

- Sexual harassment violates Title VII of the 1964 Civil Rights Act

Objective

- In this lecture, we examine the Title VII and its prohibition of sexual harassment

The law recognizes two forms of sexual harassment

Sexual harassment law is not designed to eliminate sexuality in the workplace

- The EEOC issued guidelines to use to help determine when sexual harassment occurs

- The intent of sexual harassment law is not that the workplace become devoid of sexuality

- Consensual relationships are not forbidden and employees may date

- It becomes a problem when the activity directed toward an employee is unwelcome

- Sexual harassment imposes terms or conditions different for one sex than the other

There are two theories of liability for sexual harassment claims

- Quid pro quo implies "this for that"

- Hostile environment is similar to other forms of harassment under Title VII

Quid pro quo sexual harassment

Quid pro quo sexual harassment involves a demand for sexual activity in exchange for workplace benefits

- Quid pro quo sexual harassment is the most obvious form of harassment

- Quid pro quo harassment is often accompanied by a paper trail

A prima facie case of quid pro quo sexual harassment requires three elements

- Prima facie case of quid pro quo sexual harassment

  1.   Unwelcome sexual advances

  2.   Submission was a term or condition of employment

3.   Submission or rejection was used as the basis for employment decision(s)

- Workplace benefit promised, given to, or withheld from harassee by harasser

- In exchange for sexual activity by harassee

- Complainant must establish that conduct was unwelcome

- Case discussion: <u>Bryson v. Chicago State University</u>, 96 F. 3d 912 (1996)

Hostile environment sexual harassment

A prima facie case of hostile environment sexual harassment requires the following

- A prima facie case for hostile work environment sexual harassment

  - He or she suffered intentional discrimination because of his/her sex.

  - The discrimination was pervasive and severe.

  - The discrimination detrimentally affected him or her.

  - The discrimination would detrimentally affect a reasonable person of the same sex.

- Management knew about the harassment, or should have known, and did nothing to stop it.

- Case discussion: <u>Meritor Savings Bank, FSB v. Vinson</u>, 477 U.S. 57 (1986)

Employers are often confused about what conduct rises to the level of hostile environment

- A finding of hostile environment sexual harassment requires more than occasional comments

- Not all conduct, even if it is offensive, will be found to create a hostile environment

- Certain types of conduct that will create a hostile environment

The plaintiff must show unwelcome activity

- The basis of hostile environment sexual harassment actions is unwanted activity

- If the activity is wanted or welcome by the complainant, there is no sexual harassment

- Courts can examine both direct and indirect actions to determine whether the activity was welcome

- Case discussion: <u>McLean v. Satellite Technology Services, Inc.</u>, 673 F. Supp. 1458 (E.D. Mo. 1987)

The standard of hostile work environment is not always clear

- Case discussion: <u>Rabidue v. Osceola Refining Co.</u>, 805 F. 2d 611 (6th Cir. 1986)

- The Supreme Court clarified the hostile work environment standard

- Men can be the victim of sexual harassment

An abusive working environment requires severe or pervasive intimidation, ridicule, or insult

- Courts must often determine whether the harassing activity was severe and pervasive enough

- The more frequent the occurrences, the more likely that the severe and pervasive requirement will be met

- Case discussion: <u>Ross v. Double Diamond, Inc.</u>, 672 F. Supp. 261 (N.D. Tx. 1987)

Courts have confronted the problem of perspective: Which perspective is used to determine severity?

- The determination was historically based upon the reasonable person standard

- Courts have increasingly used the reasonable victim standard

- Case discussion: <u>Ellison v. Brady</u>, 924 F. 2d 872 (9th Cir. 1991)

- Courts look to the perspective of a reasonable person in the plaintiff's position

- Case discussion: <u>Oncale v. Sundowner Offshore Services, Inc.</u>, 523 U.S. 75 (1998)

The distinctions between quid pro quo and hostile work environment are not always clear

- Case discussion: <u>Burlington Industries, Inc. v. Ellerth</u>, 524 U.S. 742 (1998)

- Case discussion: <u>Showalter v. Allison Reed Group, Inc.</u>, 767 F. Supp. 1205 (D.C. RI 1991)

Sexual harassment doesn't have to be about sexual activity

- While the harassment of the employee must be based upon gender, it need not involve sexual activity

- A hostile environment may be displayed through the use of derogatory terms

- Employers should not dismiss a harassment complaint simply because it does not mention sexual activity

An employer may have liability for sexual harassment

Courts have wrestled with the with the issue of employer liability for sexual harassment

- Courts have struggled to define the relevant standards of employer liability

- Employers are liable when either their supervisors or agents create a hostile environment

- In general, an employer is also liable if it

  - knew or should have known of the activity and

  - failed to take appropriate corrective action

- Employers are usually deemed to know of sexual harassment if it is:

  - openly practiced in the workplace

  - well-known among employees

  - brought to the employer's notice by a victim's filing a charge

Companies that want to manage their risk prudently must act before a problem occurs

- Companies need a comprehensive, detailed written policy on sexual harassment

- Once a company develops a sexual harassment policy, it should circulate it widely

- A company should have a grievance procedure

- A company must enforce its policy quickly, consistently, and aggressively

An employer can be liable for harassment by supervisors, coworkers, or third parties

- Employer liability may depend on whether there has been a tangible action

Supervisor toward employee (tangible employment action)

- An employer is strictly liable for the tangible acts of its supervisors

- An employer has no defense where there is a tangible act by a supervisor

- Therefore, in a quid pro quo case, the employer is always liable for the acts of its employee

Supervisor toward employee (no tangible employment action)

- If there is no tangible employment act by a supervisor, the employer is not strictly liable

- An employer can be vicariously liable if the actions by the supervisor constitute severe or pervasive sexual harassment

The employer can evade liability by proving an affirmative defense

- Affirmative defense:

  - The employer must prove that

1. the employer exercised reasonable care to prevent or correct promptly any such sexual harassment, and

2. the employee unreasonably failed to take advantage of any preventative or corrective opportunities provided by the employer or to avoid harm otherwise.

Coworker harassment

- The employer is liable

  - if the employer knew or should have known of the acts of the harasser and

  - took no immediate corrective action

Third party harassment of employee

- In general, the employer is liable

  - if the employer knew or should have known of the acts of the harasser and

  - took no immediate corrective action

There are ways for employers to avoid liability for sexual harassment claims

An employer must determine the truth of the allegations

- Managers may have difficulty have with addressing sexual harassment complaints

- Appropriate investigation will provide the employer a basis upon which to decide and how to respond

- The complainant must be informed of certain items

The employer must take immediate and appropriate corrective action to remedy sexual harassment

- The most appropriate remedy depends upon the facts

- The remedy must be calculated to stop the harassment and not have the effect of punishing the victim

Victims of sexual harassment may also seek other civil remedies

- Tort law provides for remedies for certain acts of sexual harassment

- A number of torts can occur as a result of sexual harassment

  - Assault

  - Battery

  - Intentional infliction of emotional distress

  - False imprisonment

  - Tortious interference with contract

- An employer may have indirect or direct liability under a tort theory

- Harassment could even be the basis for criminal prosecution

Conclusion

- The law recognizes two forms of sexual harassment

- An employer may have liability for sexual harassment

- There are other considerations in regard to sexual harassment claims

13. National origin discrimination

Introduction

Setting

- There are two trends in cases alleging national origin discrimination

- National origin claims are increasingly brought as race claims

- Language claims are brought as national origin claims

- Any employment decision based on national origin is illegal

Objective

- In this lecture, we examine national origin discrimination under Title VII

Language issues may reveal discrimination based on national origin

Accent discrimination may be an issue

- The test is whether the accent materially interferes with the ability to perform job duties

- There is a difference between a discernible foreign accent and one that interferes with communication skills

- An employer may only base an employment decision on accent if

- effective oral communication in English is required to perform job duties and

- the individual's foreign accent materially interferes with his or her ability to communicate orally in English

- Case discussion: <u>Carino v University of Oklahoma</u>, 750 F. 2d 815 (10th Cir. 1984)

Fluency requirements may indicate national origin discrimination

- A fluency requirement is permissible only if required for the effective performance of the position for which it is imposed

- The employer should not require a greater degree of fluency than is necessary for the relevant position

- Fluency requirements may lead to a hostile environment claim

- Foreign language fluency may be a requirement

English-Only rules may indicate national origin discrimination

- Some employers have instituted policies prohibiting communication in languages other than English

- An English-only rule may only be adopted for nondiscriminatory reasons

- An English-only rule is justified by business necessity if it is needed for an employer to operate safely or efficiently

- Case discussion: <u>Garcia v. Spun Steak Co.</u>, 998 F. 2d 1480 (9th Cir. 1993)

Title VII provides a remedy for harassment based on national origin

- Harassment is one of the most common claims raised in national origin charges filed with the EEOC

- The last decade saw an increase in the number of private sector national origin harassment charges filed with the EEOC

- Thirty percent of all private sector national origin charges included a harassment claim

Title VII prohibits harassment on the basis of national origin

National origin harassment violates Title VII when

- it is so severe or pervasive …

- that the individual being harassed reasonably finds …

- the work environment to be hostile or abusive.

Harassment based on national origin can take different forms

- A hostile environment may be created by the actions of supervisors, coworkers, or even nonemployees

- Relevant factors in evaluating harassment include any of the following:

  - Whether the conduct was physically threatening or intimidating

  - How frequently the conduct was repeated

  - Whether the conduct was hostile or patently offensive

  - The context in which the harassment occurred

  - Whether management responded appropriately when it learned of the harassment

Employers and employees each play a role in preventing national origin harassment

- Failure to take appropriate steps to prevent or correct harassment make an employer liability for unlawful harassment

- Failure by an employee to take reasonable steps to report harassment may prevent holding an employer responsible

- Case discussion: <u>Kang v. U. Lim America, Inc.</u>, 296 F. 3d 810 (9th Cir. 2002)

Unlawful harassment by a supervisor will make an employer liable unless it can show the following:

- The employer exercised reasonable care to prevent and correct promptly any harassing behavior, and

- The employee unreasonably failed to take advantage of any preventive or corrective opportunities provided by the employer

- The adverse employment action must be related to the harassment

- Case discussion: <u>Efrain Cruz v. John-Jay Corporation</u>, Inc, 2006 U.S. Dist. LEXIS 79621 (ND Ind)

National origin claims may involve citizenship issues

Discrimination based on citizenship may violate Title VII's prohibition against national origin discrimination

- Title VII prohibits discrimination against employees regardless of citizenship

- Citizenship discrimination may or may not violate Title VII

- Individuals who are not U.S. citizens may have claims under other federal statutes

  - Immigration Reform and Control Act of 1986

  - Fair Labor Standards Act

  - Special Visa Programs

Conclusion

- Title VII prohibits any employment decision based on national origin

- Title VII provides a remedy for harassment based on national origin

- National origin claims may involve language issues

- National origin claims may involve citizenship issues

14. Age discrimination

Introduction

Setting

- American culture values youth

- By 2030 the number of workers 65 and over will more than double

- Incorporating older workers will be a challenge for employers in the future

- Age discrimination will be the next major area of conflict

Objective

- In this lecture, we examine the Age Discrimination in Employment Act

The Age Discrimination in Employment Act regulates age discrimination

There are many misperceptions in the marketplace regarding older workers

- Statistics show that older workers are more reliable, harder working, more committed and have less absenteeism than younger workers

- Nevertheless, many in the workplace don't see it that way

- Many employers feel older employees may be more expensive to retain

- Examples of when age discrimination can occur in the workplace:

  - Hiring, forced retirement, firing

  - Job advertisements and recruitment

  - Compensation, pay, regular and fringe benefits

  - Waivers of the right to sue in exchange for severance pay

In 1967, Congress enacted the Age Discrimination in Employment Act ("ADEA")

- The statute was designed to promote employment of older persons on the basis of ability

- The law forbids discrimination when it comes to any aspect of employment

- Age discrimination involves treating an applicant or employee less favorably because of age

The Act applies to employment by public and private employers with more than 20 employees

- The Act protects employees over forty years old from discrimination

- It does not protect workers under the age of forty

- There is no claim for "reverse discrimination" under the ADEA

- It is not illegal for an employer to favor an older worker over a younger one

- Discrimination can occur when the victim and the person who discriminated are both over 40

There are similarities and differences between ADEA and Title VII

- Both are enforced by the EEOC, as well as through private actions

- Discrimination based on age is more difficult to establish than a Title VII claim

- Intent must be proved for an age discrimination claim

- The ADEA allows employers greater latitude than Title VII in the reasons for an adverse employment decision

ADEA Plaintiffs may prove their case through either disparate treatment or disparate impact

The Employee's Prima Facie Case: Disparate Treatment

- The age discrimination prima facie case is similar to Title VII

  - The plaintiff must prove that she was in the protected class

  - She must have suffered an adverse employment action

  - The plaintiff was qualified for the position

  - The plaintiff must show that he was treated differently than others outside the protected class

- The mixed-motive analysis is not relevant to an ADEA age discrimination claim

- Case discussion: Gross v. FBL Financial Services, 129 S. Ct. 2343 (2009)

If the employee makes a prima facie case, the burden of proof shifts to the employer

- The employer may establish a legitimate nondiscriminatory reason for its actions

- The ADEA provides for a bona fide occupational qualification defense

- Age is one of the most consistently applied BFOQs

- The employer's proof of a bona fide occupational qualification under the ADEA is different than Title VII

- Title VII requires that the employer demonstrate that

  - the essence of the business requires the exclusion of the members of a protected class

  - all or substantially all of the members of that class are unable to perform adequately in the position in question

Under the ADEA, the employer must prove

- The age limit is reasonably necessary to the essence of the employer's business; and either

  - All or substantially all of the individuals over that age are unable to perform the job's requirements adequately; or

  - Some of the individuals over that age possess a disqualifying trait that cannot be ascertained except by reference to age

- This third element allows an employer to exclude older workers from a position that may be safe to some older workers

- Case discussion: Western Air Lines, Inc. v. Criswell, 472 U.S. 400 (1985)

- Congress has prohibited mandatory retirement ages for most workers

Employee's Prima Facie Case: Circumstances Involving Claims of Disparate Impact

- An ADEA plaintiff may establish a claim based on disparate impact

- Courts view statistical based disparate impact claims with skepticism

- Disparate impact claims filed under the ADEA require proof of discriminatory motive

An employer's defense in an ADEA disparate impact case is likely to be RFOA

- A discriminatory policy is valid if based on a reasonable factor other than age (RFOA)

- The RFOA defense is different than the business necessity defense

- Reasonable factors other than age include economic concerns and seniority plans

Employer economic concerns may justify adverse action against older workers

- It is likely to be more expensive to maintain older workers than younger

- An objective standard must be used in determining terminations

- Courts disfavor the economic justification for the termination of older workers

- These terminations are generally legal:

  - reductions in force (RIF)

  - bankruptcy

- Other legitimate business reasons

- Case discussion: <u>Hazen Paper Co. v. Biggins</u>, 113 S.Ct. 1701 (1993)

- We have little guidance on legal effect of the correlation between age and compensation

Employee's Response: Proof of Pretext

- The employee responds by establishing that the reason or defense is pretextual

- An employee can show pretext in a number of ways

- Case discussion: <u>Pottenger v. Potlatch Corp.</u>, 329 F. 3d 740 (9th Cir. 2003)

Age discrimination raises other issues for management

Employers often encourage older workers to waive their ADEA rights

- The Older Workers Benefit Protection Act ("OWBPA") modified the ADEA

- The OWBPA concerns the legality and enforceability of early retirement incentive programs

- Employers must meet the requirements of the OWBPA in formulating waivers

- Case discussion: <u>Oubre v. Entergy Operations, Inc.</u>, 118 S.Ct. 838 (1998)

Remedies for age discrimination are limited

- Employees may receive front pay or back pay

- Compensation for pain and suffering is generally not available under the ADEA

- Forms of equitable relief include

  - Reinstatement

  - Promotions or injunctions

Conclusion

- The Age Discrimination in Employment Act regulates age discrimination

- Plaintiffs may prove their case through either disparate treatment or disparate impact

- Age discrimination raises other issues for management

15. Religious discrimination

Introduction

Setting

- Religious discrimination is different than other forms of discrimination prohibited by Title VII

- Religion is a set of beliefs, not a physical characteristic

- The law has recognized the difference in religious discrimination

- Religious discrimination can serve as a stumbling block for employers

Objective

- In this lecture, we examine Title VII's protection against religious discrimination

Title VII bans discrimination on the basis of religion

The role of religion in American life

- Many settlers in the early United States were religious dissenters

- The Second Great Awakening increased religion's role in political affairs

- Theory of manifest destiny further integrated religion into American politics

Religious organizations are generally exempt from the prohibitions in Title VII

- Case discussion: <u>Corporation of the Presiding Bishop of the Church of Jesus Christ of Latter-day Saints v. Amos</u>, 483 U.S. 327 (1987)

- Case discussion: <u>Spencer v. World Vision, Inc.</u>, 633 F. 3d 723 (9th Cir. 2010)

- The ministerial exemption prevents interference with church employment

- Case discussion: <u>McClure v. Salvation Army</u>, 460 F. 2d 553 (5th Cir.1972)

Religion can serve as a BFOQ

- Title VII permits religion to be a bona fide occupational qualification

- Title VII specifically permits educational institutions to employ those of a particular religion

- Case discussion: <u>Pime v. Loyola University of Chicago</u>, 803 F. 2d 351 (7th Cir. 1986)

Identification of sincerely held beliefs can be problematic

"Religion? That's not a religion!"

- Originally, Title VII did not define religion

- Congress amended the statute in 1972 to say religion is:

> " ... all aspects of religious observance and practice, as well as belief ..."

- Religious status is based on two considerations

  - whether the belief is closely held

  - whether it takes the place of religion in the employee's life

- The religious belief need not be a belief in a religious deity as we generally know it

- The employer cannot question the sincerity of the belief merely because it appears to be unorthodox

- The employer cannot take an adverse employment action against the employee if the employer objects to the belief

- Case discussion: <u>Peterson v. Wilmur Communs., Inc.</u>, 205 F. Supp. 2d 1014 (E.D. Wisc. 2002)

Personal preferences can be distinguished from religious beliefs

- Employees will sometimes request an accommodation for a personal preference in exercising their religion

- Case discussion: <u>Brown v. Pena</u>, 441 F. Supp. 1382 (D.C. Fla. 1997)

- An employee may not transmute political or other nonreligious views into a claim of a sincerely held religious belief

Proving a case of religious discrimination is different because of the duty to accommodate

- The law provides two means of bringing a claim for religious discrimination

- An employee can bring a claim that the employer treated him differently because of religion

- An employee can bring a claim that the employer failed to accommodate his religion

Disparate treatment analysis requires different treatment because of religion

- The prima facie case of disparate treatment based on religion is the same as for other Title VII classes

- Case discussion: <u>Campos v. City of Blue Springs</u>, 289 F. 3d 546 (8th Cir. 2002)

- The employer defends by citing LNDR or BFOQ

- Case discussion: <u>Sharon Adelman Reyes v. St. Xavier University</u>, 500 F. 3d 662 (7th Cir. 2007)

Religious discrimination is distinguished by the concept of reasonable accommodation

There is not an absolute prohibition against religious discrimination

- There is no reasonable accommodation requirement for race, gender, color or national origin

- The employer and employee each have a duty to accommodate

An employee asserting a claim of religious discrimination for failure to accommodate must first establish a prima facie case

- The employee must establish that

    1. he has a bona fide religious belief that conflicts with an employment requirement;

    2. he informed the employer of this belief and requested an accommodation of it; and

    3. he was disciplined or discharged for failing to comply with the conflicting employment requirement.

- An employer may defend by

    1. showing that it offered the employee "reasonable accommodation" or

    2. that the accommodation sought cannot be accomplished without undue burden

Once an employer is aware of a religious conflict, the employer must make a good faith attempt to accommodate the conflict

- An employer is only required to accommodate a religious practice to the extent that it does not cause an undue hardship

- An employer can discriminate against an employee for religious reasons if to not do so causes the employer undue hardship

- If no accommodation can be worked out without undue hardship on the part of the employer, the employer has fulfilled its Title VII duty

- Case discussion: Goldman v. Weinberger, 475 U.S. 503 (1986)

An employer does not have to accommodate if it imposes undue hardship

- What constitutes undue hardship also varies from situation to situation

- The accommodation the employer rejects as undue hardship may not be a mere inconvenience to the employer

- Relevant factors

  - the nature of the employer's workplace

  - the type of job needing accommodation

  - the cost of the accommodation

  - the willingness of other employees to assist in the accommodation

- the possibility of transfer of the employee and its effects

- what is done by similarly situated employers

- the number of employees available for accommodation

- the burden of accommodation upon the union

The employee's obligation to cooperate does not arise until the employer shows it has taken some initial steps

- The employee must assist in the attempted accommodation

- Case discussion: Wilson v. U.S. West Communications, 58 F. 3d 1337 (8th Cir. 1995)

- Case discussion: Cloutier v. Costco Wholesale Corp., 390 F. 3d 126 (1st Cir. 2004)

If accommodation is not possible, the employer can discriminate against an employee on the basis of religion

- Every case is fact-dependent and it is hard to make a general rule

- Case discussion: <u>Williams v. Southern Union Gas Co.</u>, 529 F. 2d 483 (10th Cir. 1976)

- An employer need not accommodate everything an employee wishes to do because it is related to the employee's religion

- Case discussion: <u>Chalmers v. Tulon Company of Richmond</u>, 101 F. 3d 1012 (1996) (4th Cir. 1996)

An employer may be liable for religious harassment

- Harassment on the basis of religion is illegal under Title VII

- It is often non-religious employees who allege they are being harassed by religious employees

- How much religious practice is acceptable in the workplace?

- Case discussion: <u>Peterson v. Hewlett-Packard Co.</u>, 358 F. 3d 599 (9th Cir. 2004)

Conclusion

- Title VII bans discrimination on the basis of religion

- Identification of sincerely held beliefs can be problematic

- Proving a case of religious discrimination is different because of the duty to accommodate

16. Affirmative action

Introduction

Setting

- Affirmative action is a controversial area of employment law

- There are many misconceptions about affirmative action

- Affirmative action involves an affirmative effort to make the workplace reflective of the population

- Affirmative action is rarely mandatory

Objective

- In this lecture, we examine affirmative action and its place in employment law

Sometimes businesses need to take more than a passive approach to equal employment opportunity

What is affirmative action and why do we need it?

- Affirmative action involves an intentional effort to include those traditionally excluded in the workplace

- Affirmative action programs are not required by Title VII

- Affirmative action must be based on a finding of discrimination, underrepresentation, or a manifest imbalance in the workplace

- The phrase "affirmative action" comes from an executive order
  "The contractor will take affirmative action to ensure that applicants are employed, and that employees are treated during employment, without regard to their race, color, religion, sex, or national origin ..."

Affirmative action has always been a limited remedy

- Affirmative action regulations do not apply to every business

- Affirmative action does not require quotas

Affirmative action arises in different ways

Affirmative action arises in three ways

- Affirmative action can arise from contractual obligations with the federal government

- Affirmative action can arise as part of a judicial remedy

- Affirmative action can arise through voluntary efforts of the employer

Affirmative Action under Executive Order 11246

- Affirmative action stems from Executive Order 11246

- This program is enforced by the Office of Federal Contract Compliance Programs (OFCCP)

- EO 11246 only applies to federal government contracts

Affirmative Action Plans are based on availability

- Based on the availability of women and minorities qualified for the particular job

- Factors used to determine availability:

  - The percentage of minorities or women with requisite skills in the reasonable recruitment area

  - The percentage of minorities or women among those promotable, transferable, and trainable within the contractor's organization

- A placement goal is not a quota

- The regulations also require corporate management compliance evaluations

Judicial Affirmative Action

- Affirmative action may be a remedy for a Title VII violation

- There are no specific requirements regarding a judicial affirmative action

- Case discussion: Local 28, Sheet Metal Workers v. EEOC, 478 U.S. 421 (1986)

Voluntary Affirmative Action

- An employer may take proactive measures to avoid discrimination claims

- Case discussion: United Steelworkers of America, AFL-CIO v. Weber, 443 U.S. 193 (1979)

- The employer may create a voluntary affirmative action plan

The Supreme Court has adopted a three-part test to determine if a voluntary affirmative action plan is valid

- First: The purposes of the plan must mirror the remedial purposes of Title VII to end discrimination

- Second: the voluntary affirmative action plan cannot "unnecessarily trammel" the interests of non-minority employees

- Third: the plan must be a temporary measure meant to eliminate imbalance and not to maintain a balance

- An affirmative action plan is different from a "diversity" plan

- Case discussion: Hopwood v. Texas, 78 F. 3d 932 (5th Cir. 1996)

- Case discussion: Grutter v. Bollinger, 539 U.S. 306 (2003)

An affirmative action plan may not use quotas

- Case discussion: Regents of the University of California v Bakke, 438 U.S. 265 (1978)

- Such plans should not displace nonminority employees

- Case discussion: Gratz v. Bollinger, 123 S.Ct. 2411 (U.S. 2003)

Reverse Discrimination

- Reverse discrimination is often considered the flip side of affirmative action

- Case discussion: Taxman v. Board of Education, 91 F. 3d 1547 (3d Cir. 1996)

- Reverse discrimination accounts for only about 3 percent of charges filed with EEOC

Conclusion

- Businesses need to take more than a passive approach to equal employment opportunity

- Affirmative action arises in three ways

- Companies should be mindful of reverse discrimination issues

17. Disability discrimination

Introduction

Setting

- Disability discrimination is often a hidden form of discrimination

- Prior to legislation, employers consistently refused to hire individuals with disabilities

- Accommodating disabilities costs money

- Without regulation, employers were not willing to bear that burden

Objective

- In this lecture, we examine the Americans with Disabilities Act and its regulation of disability discrimination

The regulation of disability discrimination has a long history

Congress first addressed disability discrimination in 1973

- Congress enacted the Vocational Rehabilitation Act of 1973

- The VRA required federal contractors to take affirmative action to employ and promote qualified disabled individuals

The Americans with Disabilities Act became effective in 1992

- The impact of the ADA has been less than its advocates hoped for

- In 2008, Congress attempted to strengthen the ADA

- The ADA Amendment Act (ADAAA) was passed to clarify and broaden the definition of disability and increase the coverage of the ADA

The ADA protects the disabled from three types of barriers

- Intentional discrimination for reasons of social bias

- Neutral standards with disparate impact on the disabled

- Discrimination as a result of barriers to job performance

Proving the case for disability discrimination

The plaintiff must first make the prima facie case

- There are four elements to the prima facie case

    - He or she is disabled

    - He or she is otherwise qualified for the position

    - The disability can be reasonably accommodated

    - He or she suffered an adverse employment decision

"He or she is disabled"

- The ADA defines disability as

    - a physical or mental impairment that substantially limits one or more of the major life activities of an individual;

    - a record of having such impairment;

- or being regarded as having such an impairment.
- The definition of disability thus has three elements:

  1. impairment;

  2. major life activity; and

  3. substantial limitation

What is a "physical or mental impairment?"

- Impairment is a broad term
- Don't mistake diagnosis for disability
- Substantially limited" is the test for disability

The impairment must substantially limit one or more of major life activities

- Court decisions have attempted to define major life activity and substantially limited
- Positive effects of mitigating measures should not be considered in determining substantial limitation

"Major life activity" is not defined in the ADA

- Major life activities are activities that the average person can perform with little or no difficulty
- Having a record of an impairment may lead to a finding of disability
- Case discussion: School Bd. of Nassau County v. Arline, 107 S.Ct. 1123 (1987)

The ADA definition of "disability" includes perception of others

- A person may have a disability if his impairment is treated as such

- The ADAAA expanded the definition of "regarded as"

- Did the employer treat the individual differently as a result of his or her assumed impairment?

- There are certain predictable assessments that in virtually all cases will indicate protection by the ADAAA

Mental or emotional impairments

- Mental impairments (intellectual disabilities) are a concern to employers

- Employers should have a process in place

- What to do about an inability to get along with others?

"Substantially limits" is not defined by the statute

- What does substantial mean?

- In 2011, the EEOC issued new rules of construction for courts to follow in determining "substantially limits"

- An impairment's impact need not be permanent to be a disability

- Recent EEOC regulations make it clear that disability should be construed broadly

"He or she is otherwise qualified for the position"

- The essential functions of the position are important

- An employer may not terminate or refuse to hire an employee who is "otherwise qualified"

- An employer must determine the essential elements of each position within a firm

- There are some things that an employer cannot consider

- The ADAAA prohibits the use of a test to determine "otherwise qualified" based on uncorrected disability

"Essential functions"

- The Acts require a determination of essential functions

- The term "essential" refers to those tasks which are fundamental

- Employers may not include in their job descriptions incidental responsibilities

- Case discussion: <u>Pickens v. Soo Line Railroad Co.</u>, 264 F. 3d 773 (8th Cir. 2001)

"The disability can be reasonably accommodated"

- Reasonable accommodation generally means the removal of unnecessary restrictions or barriers

- Reasonable accommodation does not place an undue burden or hardship on the employer

Undue burden or hardship

- Undue burden or hardship is not limited to financial difficulty

- Some examples of "undue hardship" are not acceptable defenses to a claim of discrimination

- Case discussion: <u>Cassidy v. Detroit Edison Company</u>, 138 F. 3d 629 (6th Cir. 1997)

- The employee should engage in an "interactive process"

"He or she suffered an adverse employment decision"

- Employers have a number of considerations in regard to disability discrimination

- No one yet knows the impact of the ADAAA

- Likely outcomes

    - Disability discrimination claims will no longer focus as intently on whether an employee is covered

    - Cases will focus on whether the employee and employer properly engaged in the interactive process

    - And whether a reasonable accommodation was provided (and if not, why?)

Employers have additional responsibilities in connection with health-related issues

The common law may be involved as well

- An employer's actions may result in a tort claim by the employee

- An employer may owe a common-law tort duty for the protection of co-workers

The Genetic Information Nondiscrimination Act went into effect in 2010

- Title II of GINA applies to employers

- GINA limits employers use of genetic information in three ways

- Prohibits employers from using genetic information to make employment decisions

- Restricts employers from acquiring genetic information about employees and applicants

- Requires employers to keep genetic information confidential

- GINA leaves certain questions unanswered

Conclusion

- Disability discrimination regulation has a long history

- There are requirements to prove the case for disability discrimination

- Employers have a number of considerations in regard to disability discrimination

18. Whistleblowing and antiretaliation protections

Introduction

Setting

- It is natural to want to strike back

- Winning the battle can mean losing the war

- The law protects people who use their statutorily granted rights

- The law protects people who report employer misdeeds

Objective

- In this lecture, we examine the protections that the law provides to promote socially valued activity

Employers cannot retaliate against those who take advantage of statutorily protected rights

Title VII contains an anti-retaliation provision

- The anti-retaliation provision protects anyone who engages in a "protected activity"

- The anti-retaliation provision prohibits any employer action that "well might have dissuaded a reasonable worker from making or supporting a charge of discrimination."

- Retaliation for the filing of a discrimination claim is discriminatory

- It does not matter if the underlying claim lacks merit

Analysis of a retaliation claim follows a similar analytical framework

- Retaliation cases involve the same burden-shifting analysis

- First, the plaintiff makes a prima facie case

- The elements of a prima facie case are

  - engagement in a protected activity

  - adverse employment action

  - causal connection between the two

- The employer may then give a legitimate reason for its action

- The burden shifts back to the employee to show pretext

The Supreme Court recently expanded the scope of who can make a retaliation claim

- The Supreme Court broadened the coverage of retaliation claims to include employees who themselves do not engage in "protected activity"

- Case discussion: Thompson v. North American Stainless, 131 S.Ct. 863 (2011)

- The court failed to identify a fixed class of relationships for which third-party reprisals are unlawful

Proving the retaliation claim

Engagement in protected activity

- The retaliation must be tied to a statutorily protected activity

- Perceived participation is not protected

- There must be a reasonable belief that the conduct being protested is in violation of Title VII

- A retaliation cause of action exists under section 1981

Adverse employment action

- Historically, courts were strict about what it took to constitute an adverse employment action

  - "plaintiff must show that a reasonable employee would have found the challenged action materially adverse"

- Case discussion: <u>Burlington Northern & Santa Fe Ry. v. White</u>, 548 U.S. 53 (2006)

- The Court made three important explanatory points:

  - it is important to distinguish "significant from trivial" harms;

  - it used the phrase "reasonable employee" to make clear that the standard is an objective, rather than subjective one; and

  - it defined the standard in general terms because the decision as to whether it is an adverse action must be decided in context.

Causal connection between the protected activity and the adverse employment action

- Timing is important in establishing the causation element for the prima facie case

- Often at issue is the lack of knowledge of protected activity by the decision maker

- Counterclaim against employee is not retaliation as a matter of law

The employer may establish a legitimate business reason for its action

- The employer must articulate a legitimate, nondiscriminatory reason for its action

- Case discussion: Patrick v. Ridge, 394 F. 3d 311 (5th Cir. 2004)

- Following a neutral policy is evidence that retaliation was not a motive

The employee may rebut by establishing pretext

- Evidence of failure to follow personnel policy of progressive discipline is an indicator of retaliation

- A mixed-motive analysis might be required

The law may protect an employee where the discharge violates a recognized public policy

Public policy concerns the social, moral, and economic values of a society

- Employers and society may sometimes have competing interests

- What constitutes a violation of public policy?

- Certain acts or contracts are said to be against public policy if they tend to

  - promote breach of the law,

- promote breach of the policy behind a law,

- or tend to harm the state or its citizens

Employers may not fire an employee for refusing to commit an illegal act

- Issues may arise when employees engage in conduct that may be socially desirable but not protected by law

- An employee may be protected from discharge for whistleblowing

- The federal whistleblower statute protects certain employees

- A number of states have enacted whistleblowing statutes

- The Sarbanes-Oxley Act provides protection to whistleblowers

Conclusion

- Employers cannot retaliate against those who take advantage of statutorily protected rights

- The retaliation claim follows a burden-shifting analysis

- The law may protect an employee where the discharge violates a recognized public policy

19. Restrictions on employee mobility

Introduction

Setting

- The hiring process is difficult

- Employers invest a great deal in finding their employees

- Employers would like to retain employees

- Employees are interested in retaining the freedom to change jobs

Objective

- In this lecture, we examine the means that employers use to retain employees

Most employers will seek to retain employees

Many employers will insist that employees sign some form of noncompete agreement

- The noncompete has many names

- The noncompete agreement restricts what an employee can do AFTER he leaves his employment

Historically, courts do not like noncompete agreements

- Once, courts refused to enforce noncompete agreements

- A focus on "freedom of contract" changed the manner of dealing with noncompete agreements

- The industrial revolution saw the first routine enforcement of noncompete agreements

- Under this approach, an employer had a right to protect its interests

- Courts recognized the rights of the parties to contract to whatever they wanted to contract to

What is a noncompete agreement?

- A noncompete agreement is an agreement in which an employee agrees to not compete with his employer after employment ends

- The noncompete agreement adds limitations to an employment contract

- Noncompete agreements are generally used in two different situations

  - after termination of employment

  - in conjunction with the sale of a business

Employers use different forms of contractual agreement to reach the same result

- Noncompete agreements

- Nonsolicitation agreements

- Trade secrets agreements

The common law approach to noncompete agreements is based on reasonableness

Does the noncompete agreement serve a legitimate business purpose?

- The common law seeks to balance interests
    - the interests of the employer
    - the interests of the employee
    - the interests of society
- Traditionally, the courts recognized two primary interests as legitimate justifications for a noncompete agreement
    - the employer's interests in protecting the goodwill of the business
    - the employer's interests in protecting the trade secrets of the business
- Noncompete agreements are often seen as added protection to a confidentiality agreement
- Case note: BDO Seidman v. Hirshberg

Noncompete agreements often contain four separate yet intermingled clauses

- These clauses are:
    - general non-competition
    - customer non-solicitation
    - employee non-solicitation
    - non-disclosure agreements
- Enforcement of a noncompete agreement varies from state to state

To be enforceable, the noncompete agreement must be restricted

- Restricted by time

- Restricted by geographic location

- Restricted by scope

Enforcement of a noncompete agreement is a matter of state law

State law differs greatly in its treatment of noncompete agreements

- Some states enforce all reasonable noncompete agreements

- Some states refuse to enforce noncompete agreements

- Some states utilize the 'blue pencil doctrine' to modify agreements

- An argument for abandoning the 'blue pencil' doctrine exists

In recent years, courts in enforcement states have relaxed restrictions

- Courts have broadened the interests that legitimately can be protected by employee noncompete agreements

- Courts have broadened the scope of activities that may be restricted by noncompete agreements

- States have also enacted statutes that make it easier to enforce noncompete agreements

- State courts will often enforce a stepdown provision

Even without a noncompete, a court can sometime enjoin a former employee from working for a competitor

- The "inevitable disclosure" doctrine

- Case discussion: <u>IBM v. Johnson</u>, 629 F. Supp. 2d 321 (S.D. New York 2009)

- The common law duty of loyalty

What are the ramifications of widespread use of the noncompete agreement?

- Does legal infrastructure determine a region's economy?

- Several studies suggest that the noncompete agreement is actually a drag on a state's economy

Drafting an enforceable noncompete agreement

- Identify the parties and the interest being served

- Create reasonable restrictions on scope, geography, and time

- Include a stepdown agreement

- Article: <u>Restraints on employee mobility</u>

Conclusion

- Most employers will seek to retain employees by any means necessary

- The common law approach to noncompete agreements is based on reasonableness

- Enforcement of a noncompete agreement varies from state to state

20. Privacy in employment law

Introduction

Setting

- Employment law involves the balancing of interests

- Courts must balance the interests of employers, employees, and society

- Privacy is a fundamental right

- Courts struggle with balancing privacy interests in the employment context

Objective

- In this lecture, we examine an employee's right to privacy

Where do privacy rights come from?

Privacy rights may derive from multiple sources

- The Constitution protects privacy

- Federal and state statutes protect privacy

- The common law protects privacy

Privacy protections differ based on whether the employee works in the public or private sector

- Privacy rights in the private sector of employment are limited

- Public sector privacy protections may come from the Constitution

- The Fourth Amendment protects public sector employees

- The Fourth Amendment protects against unreasonable search and seizure

- Case discussion: O'Connor v. Ortega, 480 U.S. 709 (1987)

Why is there a difference between public and private sector employees?

- There are two basic distinctions

- Constitutional rights are not involved because there is no state action

- Government employees need more protection because of the amount of power the government holds

What rights does a private sector employee have?

- Private sector employees may rely on statutory law or the common law

- Some state legislatures have provided statutory protection

- Most private sector employees must depend on the common law to protect privacy rights

The common law provides a right to collect damages for invasion of privacy

Intrusion into seclusion

- Elements of an intrusion into seclusion claim

  - the defendant employer intentionally intruded into a private area

- the plaintiff was entitled to privacy in that area, and

- the intrusion would be objectionable to a person of reasonable sensitivity.

- Case discussion: <u>Smyth v. The Pillsbury Company</u>, 914 F. Supp 97 (N.D. Penn. 1996)

Public disclosure of private facts

- Elements of a public disclosure of private facts claim

  - there was an intentional or negligent public disclosure

  - of private matters, and

  - such disclosure would be objectionable to a reasonable person of ordinary sensitivities.

- Case discussion: <u>Yoder v. Ingersoll-Rand Company</u>, 31 F. Supp. 2d 565 (N.D. Ohio 1997)

Defamation

- Elements of a defamation claim

  - false and defamatory words concerning employee

  - negligently or intentionally communicated to a third party without the employee's consent (publication)

  - resulting harm to the employee defamed

- There are defenses to a defamation claim

Publication in a false light

- Elements of publication in a false light

- there was a public disclosure

- of facts that place the employee in a false light before the public

- if the false light would be highly offensive to a reasonable person, and

- if the person providing the information had knowledge of or recklessly disregarded the falsity or false light of the publication.

- Case discussion: Peoples Bank & Trust Co. v. Globe Int'l, Inc., 786 F. Supp. 791 (D. Ark. 1992)

- A false light claim resembles defamation

- Defamation must harm one's reputation; the false light tort does not

What are my employees doing? How can I find out?

Specific issues of employee privacy

- Telephone and voice mail

- Computer monitoring

- Bugging employee conversations

- Mail interception

There are privacy issues with physical searches

- Locker searches

- Office/desk searches

- Car searches

There may be privacy implications in testing

- Polygraph examinations

- Psychological and interity testing

- Drug testing

There may be privacy implications in surveillance

- Case discussion: <u>French v. United Parcel Service, Inc.,</u> 2 F. Supp. 2d 128 (D.C. Mass. 1998)

- Regulating off-duty conduct is risky

- Does the off-duty conduct impact the workplace?

Conclusion

- Privacy is a fundamental right in the United States

- Differences exist in the treatment of public and private sector employees

- An employer must choose carefully the actions it wishes to take

21. Social media and employment law

Introduction

Setting

- Social media has become part of daily life

- Social media presents unique problems for employers

- Employers are struggling with the proper response

- Employers need to develop a social media strategy

Objective

- In this lecture, we look at potential problems and proposed employer strategies

Social media is problematic

Social media is about interaction

- Social media has killed our private lives

- Our evolving notion of what is "private" has broad legal effects

- Humans are social animals

Social media use has exploded

- Technology has made communication to large numbers of people instantaneously

- Almost every employee carries a computer and a camera in their pocket

- Communication may occur without the employee's direct involvement

The use and risks of social media

- Social media use changes faster than we are able to forecast the risk

- Risk begins with individual employees but may expose employers

- Organizations may reduce risk for both individuals and the organization

- But expect the risks to evolve as well

There are three potential problems with employees' use of social media

- Disclosure of things they should not disclose

- Harming a third person with their communication

- Violating the law (intentionally or unintentionally)

There are potential employment related legal issues in conjunction with social media

An employer may be liable for hostile work environment enforcement

- Case discussion: <u>Blakey v. Continental Airlines, Inc.</u>, 751 A.2d 538 (N.J. 2000)

- Potential employer liability is based on knowledge

- An employer may be charged with knowledge (constructive knowledge)

- Case discussion: <u>Wolfe v. Fayetteville Sch. Dist</u>, 600 F. Supp. 2d 1011 (W.D. Ark. 2009)

- Employers may have a duty to monitor social media

- An employee may overcome the employer's defense by showing pretext

    - Inconsistent assessment

    - Inconsistent enforcement

An employer may be liable for a defamation claim

- Claims of defamation often arise out of online activity

- Case discussion: <u>Collins v. Purdue University et al.</u>, 703 F. Supp. 2d 862 (N.D. Ind. 2010)

- Case discussion: <u>In re Perry</u>, 423 B.R. 215 (Bkrtcy. S.D. Tex. 2010)

- A policy may help

    - a policy that makes it clear that online statements by managers do not represent the views of the employer and

    - are not part of the manager's duties should assist in arguing that the statement was not made in the course and scope of employment.

An employer may be liable for invasion of privacy

- The online disclosure of truthful but sensitive personal information may support an invasion of privacy claim

- Case discussion: <u>Yath v. Fairview Clinics, N.P.</u>, 767 N.W.2d 34 (Minn. App. 2009)

An employer may be liable for the violation of a statute

- HIPAA

- Securities regulations

- Copyright and trademark issues

What happens if you fire an employee based on social media issues?

The National Labor Relations Act may protect the terminated employee

- Employees may engage in protected discussions regarding the terms and conditions of employment.

- Case discussion: <u>Quigley v. Giblin</u>, 569 F. 3d 449 (D.C. Cir. 2009)

The common law may protect the terminated employee

- An employer may also face an invasion of privacy claim based on the employer's review of an employee's electronic activity.

- Case discussion: <u>Quon v. City of Ontario, et al.</u>, 529 F. 3d 892 (9th Cir. 2009)

Title VII may protect the terminated employee

- Discipline against an employee based on membership in protected classes is illegal

- Employers should be careful of religious claims

A flexible social media policy can be beneficial

How can an employer protect itself?

- An employer may be liable for its employee's acts

- Under certain circumstances, an employer may be limited in its ability to discipline its employees for social media use

- An employer should develop social media strategies

Keep federal and state law in mind

- Be mindful of the provisions of the National Labor Relations Act

- Some states have limiting an employer's ability to terminate an employee based on lawful activity

  - conducted outside of working hours and

  - away from the employer's premises

Drafting a social media policy

- Encourage respectful use of social media by all employees

- Address different expectations for work hours and non-work hours

- Address use of company resources and time

- Eliminate or reduce expectation of privacy

- Reinforce nature of confidentiality obligations

- Address manager use issues

- Provide a complaint system

- Outline potential discipline

Conclusion

- Social media is problematic

- There are potential employment related legal issues

- A flexible social media policy can be beneficial

Supplemental reading

Article: Defining employee status

The importance of correctly defining employee status

Workers may be classified as employees or independent contractors. As employers increasingly rely on persons other than full-time employees to reduce the financial burden of employment, the line between employees and independent contractors has become blurred.

There are a number of reasons why employers would prefer to classify workers as independent contractors. An employer that uses independent contractors, rather than employees, eliminates many regulatory difficulties.

Classification of workers as employees makes those workers subject to many federal and state statutes governing employment. An employer has a duty to withhold taxes from employees; he has no such obligation to withhold taxes from contractors. An employer must make social security contributions on behalf of his employees. An employer must pay unemployment tax on wages paid to an employee. No corresponding obligation exists to pay similar taxes for an independent contractor. Moreover, an employer is open to discrimination suits from its employees, based on Title VII of the Civil Rights Act of 1964, the Americans with Disabilities Act, and the Age Discrimination in Employment Act. Independent contractors do not have rights under any of these statutes.

Therefore, a strong financial incentive exists to classify workers as independent contractors rather than employees. However, employers should take great care with this decision. If the employer incorrectly classifies its workers as independent contractors, risks may include state and federal tax liabilities and penalties, workers' compensation penalties, unemployment insurance penalties, wage and hour liabilities and penalties, and possibly attorneys' fees and costs. Worker misclassification can result in substantial liability for unpaid wages, and taxes, penalties and fines, among other consequences.

Federal legislation could further complicate matters. Although defeated, it is possible that the Employee Misclassification Prevention Act (H.R. 5107/S. 3254)[1] could resurface. The proposed act has several important provisions. It clarified that misclassifications are a prohibited act under the

---

[1] Employee Misclassification Prevention Act, http://www.govtrack.us/congress/bill.xpd?bill=s111-3254.

FLSA. The proposed legislation also increased penalties under appropriate circumstances and required the U.S. Department of Labor (DOL), and the states to work together to better detect misclassification. In addition, the bill would: (1) require employers to designate on their employee's records whether they are an "employee" or "independent contractor;" (2) require employers to notify workers of that classification and their right to challenge it; and (3) require state unemployment insurance agencies to audit employers to identify employers who are misclassifying employees.[2]

Preventing misclassification of employee status

The risk of misclassification is great because no bright line test exists that will accurately provide the answer as to whether an individual is an employee or independent contractor. The determination of employee status is a question of fact and depends on the particular circumstances. For that reason, it is very difficult to predict how a court or administrative agency might rule on a particular set of facts and circumstances. It is impossible to state how much weight the court or agency will give to any single factor. In some cases, a subsequent review by a court, occurring months or years after the decision was made, may determine that the classification decision was erroneous.

To make matters more complicated, determining whether a worker should be classified as an employee or an independent contractor may depend on which entity is making the classification. It is possible that state regulators examining whether a worker is entitled to unemployment compensation may determine that a worker is an independent contractor under state law while the IRS may decide the worker is an employee entitled to participate in the company retirement plan under the Employee Retirement Income Security Act (ERISA).

Employee or independent contractor?

So, how is a person to understand whether his worker is an independent contractor or employee? First, the bad news — there is no bright line rule that will state definitively what the status of the worker is. It does not matter what the employer and employee call themselves. The employment relationship may exist regardless of how it is labeled.[3] The substance of the relationship, not the label, governs the worker's status.

---

[2] Id.

[3] Publication 15-A (2011), Employer's Supplemental Tax Guide, http://www.irs.gov/publications/p15a/index.html.

No single test exists which would indicate that a worker is definitively an employee or independent contractor. Instead, courts and administrative agencies use one of three different tests to determine employee status.

The common law agency test

Perhaps the most used test is known as the common law agency test. The EEOC and the majority of appellate districts use some version of the common law agency test.[4] The Supreme Court described this test in Community for Creative Non-Violence v. Reid[5] and Nationwide Mut. Ins. Co. v. Darden.[6] In Darden, the U.S. Supreme Court was required to interpret the ERISA definition of employer. The text of the statute proved to be of little use. Section 3(6) of ERISA defines "employee" as "any individual employed by an employer." The Supreme Court applied the common law test. As rationale, the Court explained its reasoning for applying the common law agency test to the definition of the term "employee":

> [w]here Congress uses terms that have accumulated settled meaning under ... the common law, a court must infer, unless the statute otherwise dictates, that Congress means to incorporate the established meaning of these terms.... In the past, when Congress has used the term 'employee' without defining it, we have concluded that Congress intended to describe the conventional master-servant relationship as understood by common-law agency doctrine.[7]

---

[4] The EEOC applies this test in ADA, ADEA and Title VII cases. See, EEOC Compliance Manual, Section 2 Threshold Issues at footnote 71 ("The Darden rationale applies under the EEO statutes because the ERISA definition of 'employee' is identical to that in Title VII, the ADEA, and the ADA."); 1st Circuit: Alberty-Vélez v. Corporación de Puerto Rico Para La Difusión Pública, 361 F.3d 1 (1stCir. 2004)(Title VII action); Dykes v. DePuy, Inc., 140 F.3d 31 (1st Cir. 1998)(ADA action); and Speen v. Crown Clothing Corp., 102 F.3d 625 (1st Cir. 1996)(ADEA action); 2d Circuit: Eisenberg v. Advance Relocation & Storage, Inc., 237 F.3d 111 (2d Cir. 2000)(Title VII action); 3d Circuit: No cases found adopting any of the three tests; 4thCircuit: Farlow v. Wachovia Bank of North Carolina, N.A., 259 F.3d 309 (4th Cir. 2001)(Title VII action);6th Circuit: Weary v. Cochran, 377 F.3d 522 (6thCir. 2004)(ADEA action); Shah v. Deaconess Hosp., 355 F.3d 496 (6th Cir. 2004)(Title VII action); andJohnson v. City of Saline, 151 F.3d 564 (6th Cir. 1998)(ADA action); 8th Circuit: Wojewski v. Rapid City Regional Hosp., Inc., 450 F.3d 338 (8th Cir. 2006) (Rehabilitation Act); Wortham v. American Family Ins. Group, 385 F.3d 1139 (8th Cir. 2004)(ADEA and Title VII action); and Lerohl v. Friends of Minnesota Sinfonia, 322 F.3d 486 (8th Cir. 2003)(ADA and Title VII action); 9th Circuit: Barnhart v. New York Life Ins. Co., 141 F.3d 1310 (9th Cir. 1998)(ADEA action).

[5] 490 U.S. 730 (1989).

[6] 112 S.Ct. 1344 (1992).

[7] Darden, 112 S.Ct. at 1348.

The centerpiece of the common law test is the concept of right of control. Where a worker--rather than the company--controls where, when and how the work is performed, the more likely an independent contractor relationship exists. Similarly, individuals who can work for other clients and can subcontract their work are more likely to be classified as independent contractors. Nevertheless, one may not simply determine whether or not the employer has the right of control over the work of the putative employee. Instead, the Court named thirteen factors that constituted a non-exhaustive list of factors to consider when applying the common law agency test:

1. The hiring party's right to control the manner and means by which the product is accomplished.

2. The skill required.

3. The source of the instrumentalities and tools.

4. The location of the work.

5. The duration of the relationship between the parties.

6. Whether the hiring party has the right to assign additional projects to the hired party.

7. The extent of the hired party's discretion over when and how long to work.

8. The method of payment.

9. The hired party's role in hiring and paying assistants.

10. Whether the work is part of the regular business of the hiring party.

11. Whether the hiring party is in business.

12. The provision of employee benefits.

13. The tax treatment of the hired party.

Moreover, employers cannot rely on one factor more than any other. "Since the common-law test contains no shorthand formula or magic phrase that can be applied to find the answer, . . . all of the incidents of the relationship must be assessed and weighed with no one factor being decisive."[8]

The economic realities test

The other dominant employee status test is known as the economic realities test. In Worth v. Tyer, 276 F.3d 249, 263 (7th Cir. 2001), the Seventh Circuit set forth the five factors comprising the economic realities test:

1. [T]he extent of the employer's control and supervision over the worker, including directions on scheduling and performance of work,

2. the kind of occupation and nature of skill required, including whether skills are obtained in the workplace,

3. responsibility for the costs of operation, such as equipment, supplies, fees, licenses, workplace, and maintenance of operations,

4. method and form of payment and benefits, and

5. length of job commitment and/or expectations.

For the economic realities test, the employer's right to control the worker's actions remains the most important factor. "If an employer has the right to control and direct the work of an individual, not only as to the result to be achieved, but also as to the details by which that result is achieved, an employer/employee relationship is likely to exist." Worth at 263, quoting Spirides v. Reinhardt, 613 F.2d 826, 831-32 (D.C.Cir.1979).

Two circuits follow the economic realities test.[9]

---

[8] Darden, 112 S.Ct. at 1349.

[9] 7th Circuit: Worth v. Tyer, 276 F.3d 249 (7th Cir. 2001)(Title VII action); Vakharia v. Swedish Covenant Hosp., 190 F.3d 799 (7th Cir. 1999)(ADEA and Title VII action); and Aberman v. J. Abouchar & Sons, Inc., 160 F.3d 1148 (7th Cir. 1998)(ADA action); and 9th Circuit: In Adcock v. Chrysler Corp., 166 F.3d 1290 (9th Cir. 1999), the Ninth Circuit noted that the common law agency approach set forth in Darden is essentially indistinguishable from the approach previously used by this circuit in analyzing "employment relationship" for Title VII purposes; but because the case in question relies on whether the parties' agreement would have constituted an employment relationship, and not on the definition of employee, the court relies on the five factor economic realities test set forth in Lutcher v. Musicians Union Local 47, 633 F.2d 880 (9th Cir. 1980), which specifically distinguished employment from independent contractual affiliation and was not abrogated by the common law approach to defining "employee". See, Adcock, 166 F.3d 1292 at footnote 3.

The hybrid approach

The Fifth Circuit follows a hybrid approach. In a Title VII case, Arbaugh v. Y & H Corp., 380 F.3d 219, 226 (5th Cir. 2004), the Fifth Circuit defined the hybrid approach as follows:

> the most important factor is "the extent of the employer's right to control the 'means and manner' of the worker's performance." . . . The factors pertinent to this inquiry include: (1) ownership of the equipment necessary to perform the job; (2) responsibility for costs associated with operating that equipment and for license fees and taxes; (3) responsibility for obtaining insurance; (4) responsibility for maintenance and operating supplies; (5) ability to influence profits; (6) length of the job commitment; (7) form of payment; and (8) directions on schedules and on performing work.

In addition to the Fifth and Tenth Circuits, one other circuit follows the hybrid approach and one other circuit has not yet decided whether to follow the common law agency test or the hybrid approach.[10]

The IRS test

The IRS created its own test to determine employee status. Where the test once was made up of 20 different factors, it has now been simplified. To determine a worker's status, the IRS applies relevant facts into three main categories: behavioral control, financial control, and the overall view of the relationship.

B. *Behavioral Control*

Once again, the test starts with the right of control. The IRS will first determine whether the employer has a right to direct or control how the worker does the work. If the employer has the right to direct and control the worker's daily functions, the worker is likely to be deemed an employee. The important thing to remember is that it is the right to control--and not actual control--that is determinative. Even the right to direct and control the work may be enough to

---

[10] 4th Circuit: Mangram v. General Motors Corp.,108 F.3d 61, 62-63 (4th Cir. 1997)(It has adopted the same factors relied upon by the Tenth Circuit); and 11th Circuit: In Garcia v. Copenhaver, Bell & Associates, M.D.'s, P.A., 104 F.3d 1256, 1266-67 (11th Cir. 1997), the Eleventh Circuit held that it did not have to decide whether the hybrid test or the common law agency test applied to this ADEA action. However, in a non-ADEA action, the Eleventh Circuit has relied on both the hybrid test and the common law agency test. Garcia, 104 F.3d at 1266. See also, Daughtrey v. Honeywell, Inc., 3 F.3d 1488, 1495-96 (11th Cir. 1993)(declining to decide whether the common law agency test must be applied instead of the hybrid test to ADEA cases in the wake of Darden).

create an employment relationship. Important factors to consider is whether the employer instructs (or has the right to instruct) its employees in the following areas:

1. When and where to do the work;

2. How the work should be performed;

3. The acceptable standards of work performance;

4. What tools or equipment to use and where to purchase them;

5. Which individual performs various tasks; and

6. What order or sequence to follow in performing the work.

The IRS analysis will also examine the amount of training that an individual receives from the business. An individual who is trained to perform services in a particular manner is likely to be considered to be an employee. Independent contractors, on the other hand, ordinarily use their own methods and are responsible for obtaining their own specific training.

Even in the absence of instructions, a right to control may exist if the employer has the right to determine how the results are achieved.

C. Financial Control

The financial control that an employer exerts over its workers is also a key factor in determining whether an employment relationship exists. The IRS will exam the control the employer exerts over the business aspects of the worker's job under the following circumstances:

1. The worker has no expectation of realizing a profit or loss. An independent contractor can be expected to make a profit or loss.

2. By reimbursing the worker's business expenses. Independent contractors are more likely to have non-reimbursed expenses. Fixed ongoing costs that are incurred by the worker regardless of whether work is performed demonstrate that the worker operates an independent business that is subject to profits and losses.

3. The worker has no financial investment. An independent contractor often has a significant financial investment in the business he or she operates (although a significant investment is not always necessary for independent contractor status).

4. The worker does not make his or her services available to the relevant market. An independent contractor is free to seek out business opportunities and perform work

for multiple clients. They also advertise, maintain a visible business location, and are available to work in the relevant market.

5. The worker is paid based on the amount of time spent. Employees are generally guaranteed a regular wage amount that is paid on an hourly or weekly basis, even if wages are supplemented by a commission. Independent contractors, however, are usually paid a flat fee to perform or to complete a particular job (although there are some notable exceptions, such as plumbers and attorneys who are independent contractors but who are usually paid by the hour).

6. The worker is required to personally perform services. If services are required to be performed only by the worker that indicates that the worker is an employee under the direction and control of the business. Independent contractors can substitute another person's services without approval of the business.[11]

D. *Overall view of the relationship*

The IRS will also consider the overall nature of the relationship, including:

1. The intent of the parties to create either an employer/employee relationship or a principal/independent contractor relationship, as set forth in a written contract.

2. The permanency of the relationship. Engaging a worker for an indefinite period of time as opposed to a specific period of time generally indicates that an employer/employee relationship exists.

3. The right to terminate the worker at will. Having the right to terminate a worker at will – i.e., at any time, for any reason, and without notice – strongly suggests the existence of an employer/employee relationship.

4. Requirements to attend meetings or prepare reports. Unless the primary purpose of the contract is to attend meetings or prepare reports, these activities normally demonstrate an employee-employer relationship.

5. The services performed by the worker are part of the regular business of the project/department. A worker who provides services that are part of the regular business activity of the project/department is more likely to be construed as an employee. Examples: Waiters at a restaurant are considered employees because they serve food, which is an integral part of the restaurant's business. Similarly, if a grant or project has the purpose of counseling high school students, then individuals who are

---

[11] IRS Publication 15A.

engaged to counsel high school students are probably considered employees and not independent contractors.

6. Providing the worker with benefits, such as insurance, a pension plan, vacation pay, or sick pay. Traditionally, only workers with employee status receive benefits.[12]

Conclusion

Where does this leave the employer? The quick answer – when in doubt, classify them as an employee.

---

[12] IRS Publication 15A.

Case note: Ricci v. DeStefano

Editor: Griffin Pivateau
Case Name: Ricci v. DeStefano
Citation: 129 S.Ct. 2658 (2009)

Introduction:

In the fire department of New Haven, Connecticut--as in emergency-service agencies throughout the nation--firefighters prize their promotion to and within the officer ranks. An agency's officers command respect within the department and in the whole community. Of course, added responsibilities command increased salary and benefits. Aware of the intense competition for promotions, New Haven, like many cities, relies on objective examinations to identify the best qualified candidates.

In 2003, 118 New Haven firefighters took examinations to qualify for promotion to the rank of lieutenant or captain. Promotion examinations in New Haven (or City) were infrequent, so the stakes were high. The results would determine which firefighters would be considered for promotions during the next two years, and the order in which they would be considered. Many firefighters studied for months, at considerable personal and financial cost.

When the examination results showed that white candidates had outperformed minority candidates, a vigorous debate occurred between the mayor, politicians, and union officials. Some firefighters argued the tests should be discarded because the results showed the tests to be discriminatory. They threatened a discrimination lawsuit if the City made promotions based on the tests. Other firefighters said the exams were neutral and fair. These firefighters, in turn, threatened a discrimination lawsuit against the City if, out of fear because of the statistical racial disparity, ignored the test results and denied promotions to the candidates who had performed well.

In the end, the City took the side of those who protested the test results. It threw out the results of the examinations. Shortly thereafter, certain white and Hispanic firefighters, who likely would have been promoted based on their good test performance, sued the City and some of its officials.

Facts:

E. A test for promotion

When the City of New Haven undertook to fill vacant lieutenant and captain positions in its fire department (Department), the promotion and hiring process was governed by the city charter, in addition to federal and state law. The charter establishes a merit system. That system required the City to fill vacancies in certain civil-service ranks with the most qualified individuals. The most qualified individuals would be determined by job-related examinations. After each examination, the New Haven Civil Service Board (CSB) certified a ranked list of applicants who passed the test. Under the charter's "rule of three," the relevant hiring authority must fill each vacancy by choosing one candidate from the top three scorers on the list. Certified promotional lists remain valid for two years.

The City's contract with the New Haven firefighters' union specified additional requirements for the promotion process. Under the contract, applicants for lieutenant and captain positions were to be screened using written and oral examinations, with the written exam accounting for 60 percent and the oral exam 40 percent of an applicant's total score. To sit for the examinations, candidates for lieutenant needed 30 months' experience in the Department, a high-school diploma, and certain vocational training courses. Candidates for captain needed one year's service as a lieutenant in the Department, a high-school diploma, and certain vocational training courses.

After reviewing bids from various consultants, the City hired Industrial/Organizational Solutions, Inc. (IOS) to develop and administer the examinations. The City agreed to pay IOS $100,000. IOS is an Illinois company that specializes in designing entry-level and promotional examinations for fire and police departments.

In order to fit the examinations to the New Haven Department, IOS began the test-design process by performing job analyses to identify the tasks, knowledge, skills, and abilities that are essential for the lieutenant and captain positions. IOS representatives interviewed incumbent captains and lieutenants and their supervisors. They rode with and observed other on-duty officers. Using information from those interviews and ride-alongs, IOS wrote job-analysis questionnaires and administered them to most of the incumbent battalion chiefs, captains, and lieutenants in the Department. At every stage of the job analyses, IOS, by deliberate choice, oversampled minority firefighters to ensure that the results--which IOS would use to develop the examinations--would not unintentionally favor white candidates.

With the job-analysis information in hand, IOS developed the written examinations to measure the candidates' job-related knowledge. For each test, IOS compiled a list of training manuals, Department procedures, and other materials to use as sources for the test questions. IOS presented the proposed sources to the New Haven fire chief and assistant fire chief for their approval. Then, using the approved sources, IOS drafted a multiple-choice test for each position. Each test had 100 questions, as required by CSB rules, and was written below a 10th-grade reading level. After IOS prepared the tests, the City opened a 3-month study period. It gave candidates a list that identified the source material for the questions, including the specific chapters from which the questions were taken.

IOS developed the oral examinations as well. The oral exams concentrated on job skills and abilities. Using the job-analysis information, IOS wrote hypothetical situations to test incident-command skills, firefighting tactics, interpersonal skills, leadership, and management ability, among other things. Candidates would be presented with these hypotheticals and asked to respond before a panel of three assessors.

IOS assembled a pool of 30 assessors who were superior in rank to the positions being tested. At the City's insistence (because of controversy surrounding previous examinations), all the assessors came from outside Connecticut. IOS submitted the assessors' resumes to City officials for approval. They were battalion chiefs, assistant chiefs, and chiefs from departments of similar sizes to New Haven's throughout the country. Sixty-six percent of the panelists were minorities, and each of the nine three-member assessment panels contained two minority members. IOS trained the panelists for several hours on the day before it administered the examinations, teaching them how to score the candidates' responses consistently using checklists of desired criteria.

F. *The examination and its aftermath*

Candidates took the examinations in November and December 2003. Seventy-seven candidates completed the lieutenant examination--43 whites, 19 blacks, and 15 Hispanics. Of those, 34 candidates passed--25 whites, 6 blacks, and 3 Hispanics. Eight lieutenant positions were vacant at the time of the examination. As the rule of three operated, this meant that the top 10 candidates were eligible for an immediate promotion to lieutenant. All 10 were white. Subsequent vacancies would have allowed at least 3 black candidates to be considered for promotion to lieutenant.

Forty-one candidates completed the captain examination--25 whites, 8 blacks, and 8 Hispanics. Of those, 22 candidates passed--16 whites, 3 blacks, and 3 Hispanics. Seven captain positions were vacant at the time of the examination. Under the rule of three, 9 candidates were eligible for an immediate promotion to captain--7 whites and 2 Hispanics.

Beginning in January 2004, the CSB began to hold numerous meetings with city officials, firefighters, union officials and local politicians. At these meetings, the various stakeholders would provide make statements regarding the CSB's proper reaction.

At the first meeting, the director of the City's Department of Human Resources told the CSB that "there is a significant disparate impact on these two exams." She distributed lists showing the candidates' races and scores (written, oral, and composite) but not their names. The City's attorney, Thomas Ude, also described the test results as reflecting "a very significant disparate impact." Ude asked the Civil Service Bureau to refuse to certify the exam results and offered his opinion that "promotions ... as a result of these tests would not be consistent with federal law." Ude further argued that "there are much better alternatives to identifying [firefighting] skills."

The city's chief administrative officer likewise argued that certifying the exam results created a situation in which black and Hispanic candidates were disproportionately excluded from opportunity. He believed that that there were alternative means of testing and "some different ways of doing written examinations."

Although they did not know whether they had passed or failed, some firefighter-candidates spoke at the first CSB meeting in favor of certifying the test results. Michael Blatchley stated that "every one" of the questions on the written examination "came from the study material. . . . [I]f you read the materials and you studied the material, you would have done well on the test."

Frank Ricci, who would later lead the lawsuit, stated that the test questions were based on the Department's own rules and procedures and on "nationally recognized" materials that represented the "accepted standards" for firefighting. Ricci stated that he had "several learning disabilities," including dyslexia; that he had spent more than $1,000 to purchase the materials and pay his neighbor to read them on tape so he could "give it his best shot"; and that he had studied "8 to 13 hours a day to prepare" for the test. "I don't even know if I made it," Ricci told the CSB, "but the people who passed should be promoted. When your life's on the line, second best may not be good enough."

Other firefighters spoke against certifying the test results. They described the test questions as outdated or not relevant to firefighting practices in New Haven. One such firefighter, Gary Tinney, stated that the source materials "came out of New York. . . . Their makeup of their city and everything is totally different than ours." Still other firefighters criticized the test materials, a full set of which cost about $ 500, for being too expensive and too long.

A representative of IOS also spoke before the CSB. The representative explained the exam-development process to the CSB. He began by describing the job analyses IOS performed of the captain and lieutenant positions--the interviews, ride-alongs, and questionnaires IOS designed to "generate a list of tasks, knowledge, skills and abilities that are considered essential to performance" of the jobs. He outlined how IOS prepared the written and oral examinations, based on the job-analysis results, to test most heavily those qualities that the results indicated were "critical" or "essential." And he noted that IOS took the material for each test question directly from the approved source materials.

The IOS representative assured the CSB that third-party reviewers had scrutinized the examinations to ensure that the written test was drawn from the source material and that the oral test accurately tested real-world situations that captains and lieutenants would face. The representative confirmed that IOS had selected oral-examination panelists so that each three-member assessment panel included one white, one black, and one Hispanic member.

The CSB also heard from Christopher Hornick, a competitor to IOS. Although he had not reviewed the test, Hornick stated that he was "a little surprised" by the disparity in the candidates' scores. When asked to explain the New Haven test results, he suggested that the collective-bargaining agreement's requirement of using written and oral examinations with a 60/40 composite score might account for the statistical disparity. Hornick also stated that "by not having anyone from within the Department review" the tests before they were administered--a limitation the City had imposed to protect the security of the exam questions--"you inevitably get things in there" that are based on the source materials but are not relevant to New Haven. He suggested that testing candidates at an "assessment center" rather than using written and oral examinations "might serve the City's needs better." Hornick stated that assessment centers, where candidates face real-world situations and respond just as they would in the field, allow candidates "to demonstrate how they would address a particular problem as opposed to just verbally saying it or identifying the correct option on a written test."

In the end, the CSB decided not to certify the examination results. The chairman of the CSB explained that "nobody convinced me that we can feel comfortable that, in fact, there's some likelihood that there's going to be an exam designed that's going to be less discriminatory."

G. The lawsuit

The firefighter plaintiffs consisted of 17 white firefighters and 1 Hispanic firefighter. The plaintiffs were those who passed the examination but were denied a chance at promotions. They brought a disparate treatment claim, arguing that they were treated differently on the basis of race. In other words, but for their race, they would have been given an opportunity for promotion. They argued that the opportunity had been denied to them because of their race.

The City acknowledged the firefighters' argument but argued that it could not certify the exams, because to do so would result in a disparate impact claim. The City stated that it had a good faith belief that they would have violated the disparate-impact prohibition in Title VII had they certified the examination results. It follows, they maintained, that they cannot be held liable under Title VII's disparate-treatment provision for attempting to comply with Title VII's disparate-impact bar.

The firefighters replied that the City's good-faith belief was not a valid defense to allegations of disparate treatment and unconstitutional discrimination.

The trial court sided with the City. The judge stated that the City had not acted because of "discriminatory animus" toward petitioners. It concluded that respondents' actions were not "based on race" because "all applicants took the same test, and the result was the same for all because the test results were discarded and nobody was promoted."

The Court of Appeals sided with the trial court, affirming the District Court opinion.

Issue:

Can an employer engage in what would otherwise be prohibited disparate-treatment discrimination to avoid disparate-impact liability?

Analysis:

A. The applicable law:

Title VII of the Civil Rights Act of 1964 prohibits employment discrimination on the basis of race, color, religion, sex, or national origin. Title VII prohibits both intentional discrimination (known as "disparate treatment") as well as practices that are not intended to discriminate but in fact have a disproportionately adverse effect on minorities (known as "disparate impact").

As enacted in 1964, Title VII's principal nondiscrimination provision held employers liable only for disparate treatment. That section retains its original wording today.

Title VII makes it unlawful for an employer "to fail or refuse to hire or to discharge any individual, or otherwise to discriminate against any individual with respect to his compensation, terms, conditions, or privileges of employment, because of such individual's race, color, religion, sex, or national origin." Disparate-treatment cases present "the most easily understood type of discrimination," and occur where an employer has "treated [a] particular person less favorably than others because of" a protected trait. A disparate-treatment plaintiff must establish "that the defendant had a discriminatory intent or motive" for taking a job-related action.

The Civil Rights Act of 1964 did not include an express prohibition on policies or practices that produce a disparate impact. But in Griggs v. Duke Power Co., 401 U.S. 424, 91 S. Ct. 849, 28 L. Ed. 2d 158 (1971), the Court interpreted the Act to prohibit, in some cases, employers' facially neutral practices that, in fact, are "discriminatory in operation.

The Griggs Court stated that the "touchstone" for disparate-impact liability is the lack of "business necessity": "If an employment practice which operates to exclude [minorities] cannot be shown to be related to job performance, the practice is prohibited." The employer's burden is to demonstrate that practice has "a manifest relationship to the employment in question." Under those precedents, if an employer met its burden by showing that its practice was job-related, the plaintiff was required to show a legitimate alternative that would have resulted in less discrimination. Thus, a complaining party was permitted to show "that other tests or selection devices, without a similarly undesirable racial effect would also serve the employer's legitimate interest."

Twenty years after Griggs, the Civil Rights Act of 1991 was enacted. The Act included a provision codifying the prohibition on disparate-impact discrimination. That provision is now in force along with the disparate-treatment section discussed previously.

Under the disparate-impact statute, a plaintiff establishes a prima facie violation by showing that an employer uses "a particular employment practice that causes a disparate impact on the basis of race, color, religion, sex, or national origin." An employer may defend against liability by demonstrating that the practice is "job related for the position in question and consistent with business necessity." Even if the employer meets that burden, however, a plaintiff may still succeed by showing that the employer refuses to adopt an available alternative employment practice that has less disparate impact and serves the employer's legitimate needs.

B. *The reasoning of the Supreme Court*

The Supreme Court was aware that the City's actions would violate the disparate-treatment prohibition of Title VII unless there was a valid defense. The City chose not to certify the examination results because of the statistical disparity based on race--i.e., how minority candidates had performed when compared to white candidates. The Supreme Court noted that the City rejected the test results because "too many whites and not enough minorities would be promoted were the lists to be certified."

The Court stated that, unless there was some other form of justification, this "express, race-based decision making violates Title VII's command that employers cannot take adverse employment actions because of an individual's race." The City rejected the test results solely because the higher scoring candidates were white. In the minds of the Court then, the question was not whether the City's conduct was discriminatory, but whether the City had a lawful justification for its race-based action.

The court framed the issue as follows: "whether the purpose to avoid disparate-impact liability excuses what otherwise would be prohibited disparate-treatment discrimination." The court sought to provide guidance to employers and courts for situations when those two principles, disparate impact and disparate treatment, are in conflict. The court noted further that its decision must be consistent with the important purpose of Title VII--that the workplace be an environment free of discrimination, where race is not a barrier to opportunity.

The Court heard arguments from the firefighters and the City. Each party suggested the appropriate test for an employer when faced with the question of what happens when fear of disparate impact turns into disparate treatment.

The firefighter plaintiffs argued that, before it can use compliance as a defense in a disparate-treatment suit, an employer must be in violation of the disparate-impact provision. The Supreme Court declined to accept this argument, finding that it was overly simplistic and too restrictive of Title VII's purpose. The rule offered by the firefighters would run counter to what the Court recognized as Congress's intent that "voluntary compliance" be "the preferred means of achieving the objectives of Title VII." Forbidding employers to act unless they know, with certainty, that a practice violates the disparate-impact provision would bring compliance efforts to a near standstill. Even in the limited situations when this restricted standard could be met, employers likely would hesitate before taking voluntary action for fear of later being proven wrong in the course of litigation and then held to account for disparate treatment.

The City argued that an employer's good-faith belief that its actions are necessary to comply with Title VII's disparate-impact provision should be enough to justify race-conscious conduct. But the Supreme Court rejected this argument, noting that the original, foundational prohibition of Title VII bars employers from taking adverse action "because of . . . race." The Court also noted that when Congress codified the disparate-impact provision in 1991, it made no exception to disparate-treatment liability for actions taken in a good-faith effort to comply with the new, disparate-impact provision in subsection (k).

The Court reasoned that allowing employers to violate the disparate-treatment prohibition based on a mere good-faith fear of disparate-impact liability would encourage race-based action at the slightest hint of disparate impact. A minimal standard could cause employers to discard the results of lawful and beneficial promotional examinations even where there is little if any evidence of disparate-impact discrimination. That would amount to a de facto quota system, in which a "focus on statistics . . . could put undue pressure on employers to adopt inappropriate prophylactic measures." Even worse, an employer could discard test results (or other employment practices) with the intent of obtaining the employer's preferred racial balance. That operational principle could not be justified, for Title VII is express in disclaiming any interpretation of its requirements as calling for outright racial balancing. The purpose of Title VII "is to promote hiring on the basis of job qualifications, rather than on the basis of race or color."

The Court rejected the arguments of both plaintiffs and defendants. Instead, the Court held that there must be a "strong basis in evidence" of a disparate impact violation before it could take a race-conscious action. The Court found that the strong basis in evidence standard leaves room for employers' voluntary compliance efforts, which are essential to the statutory scheme and to Congress's efforts to eradicate workplace discrimination. Furthermore, the standard constrains employers' discretion in making race-based decisions: It limits that discretion to cases in which there is a strong basis in evidence of disparate-impact liability, but it is not so restrictive that it allows employers to act only when there is a provable, actual violation.

In the Ricci case, the Court found that the City was compelled to take a hard look at the examinations to determine whether certifying the results would have had an impermissible disparate impact. Nevertheless, a prima facie case of disparate-impact liability--essentially, a threshold showing of a significant statistical disparity and nothing more--is not a strong basis in evidence that the City would have been liable under Title VII had it certified the results. That is because the City could be liable for disparate-impact discrimination only if the examinations were not job related and consistent with business necessity, or if there existed an equally valid, less-discriminatory alternative that served the City's needs but that the City refused to adopt.

Conclusion:

Fear of litigation alone cannot justify the City's reliance on race to the detriment of individuals who passed the examinations and qualified for promotions. Discarding the test results was impermissible under Title VII.

Case Note: Ellison v. Brady

Editor: Griffin Pivateau
Case Name: Ellison v. Brady
Citation: 924 F.2d 872 (9th Cir. 1991)

Introduction:

Sexual harassment is an area of the law that, by its nature, is full of gray areas. In every sexual harassment lawsuit, a court must determine whether the conduct alleged fell outside the normal scope of workplace activity. If so, the court must then decide whether the activity that took place sufficiently changed the conditions of the workplace. The court must also decide whether the employer should be liable for the acts of its employees that gave rise to the charge of sexual harassment.

The facts:

Kerry Ellison worked as a revenue agent for the Internal Revenue Service in San Mateo, California. During her initial training in 1984 she met Sterling Gray, another trainee, who was also assigned to the San Mateo office. The two co-workers never became friends, and they did not work closely together.

Gray's desk was twenty feet from Ellison's desk, two rows behind and one row over. Revenue agents in the San Mateo office often went to lunch in groups. In June of 1986 when no one else was in the office, Gray asked Ellison to lunch. She accepted. Gray had to pick up his son's forgotten lunch, so they stopped by Gray's house. He gave Ellison a tour of his house.

Ellison alleges that after the June lunch Gray started to pester her with unnecessary questions and hang around her desk. On October 9, 1986, Gray asked Ellison out for a drink after work. She declined, but she suggested that they have lunch the following week. She did not want to have lunch alone with him, and she tried to stay away from the office during lunch time. Onc day during the following week, Gray uncharacteristically dressed in a three-piece suit and asked Ellison out for lunch. Again, she did not accept.

On October 22, 1986 Gray handed Ellison a note he wrote on a telephone message slip which read:

> I cried over you last night and I'm totally drained today. I have never been in such constant term oil (sic). Thank you for talking with me. I could not stand to feel your hatred for another day.

When Ellison realized that Gray wrote the note, she became shocked and frightened and left the room. Gray followed her into the hallway and demanded that she talk to him, but she left the building.

Ellison later showed the note to Bonnie Miller, who supervised both Ellison and Gray. Miller said "this is sexual harassment." Ellison asked Miller not to do anything about it. She wanted to try to handle it herself. Ellison asked a male co-worker to talk to Gray, to tell him that she was not interested in him and to leave her alone. The next day, Thursday, Gray called in sick.

Ellison did not work on Friday, and on the following Monday, she started four weeks of training in St. Louis, Missouri. Gray mailed her a card and a typed, single-spaced, three-page letter. She describes this letter as "twenty times, a hundred times weirder" than the prior note. Gray wrote, in part:

> I know that you are worth knowing with or without sex. . . . Leaving aside the hassles and disasters of recent weeks. I have enjoyed you so much over these past few months. Watching you. Experiencing you from O so far away. Admiring your style and elan. . . . Don't you think it odd that two people who have never even talked together, alone, are striking off such intense sparks . . . I will [write] another letter in the near future.

In the middle of this long letter, Gray noted, "I am obligated to you so much that if you want me to leave you alone I will. . . . If you want me to forget you entirely, I cannot do that."

Explaining her reaction, Ellison stated, "I just thought he was crazy. I thought he was nuts. I didn't know what he would do next. I was frightened."

She immediately telephoned Miller. Ellison told her supervisor that she was frightened and really upset. She requested that Miller transfer either her or Gray because she would not be comfortable working in the same office with him. Miller asked Ellison to send a copy of the card and letter to San Mateo.

Miller then telephoned her supervisor, Joe Benton, and discussed the problem. That same day she had a counseling session with Gray. She informed him that he was entitled to union representation. During this meeting, she told Gray to leave Ellison alone.

At Benton's request, Miller apprised the labor relations department of the situation. She also reminded Gray many times over the next few weeks that he must not contact Ellison in any way. Gray subsequently transferred to the San Francisco office on November 24, 1986. Ellison returned from St. Louis in late November and did not discuss the matter further with Miller.

After three weeks in San Francisco, Gray filed union grievances requesting a return to the San Mateo office. The IRS and the union settled the grievances in Gray's favor, agreeing to allow him to transfer back to the San Mateo office provided that he spend four more months in San Francisco and promise not to bother Ellison. On January 28, 1987,

Ellison first learned of Gray's request in a letter from Miller explaining that Gray would return to the San Mateo office. The letter indicated that management decided to resolve Ellison's problem with a six-month separation, and that it would take additional action if the problem recurred.

After receiving the letter, Ellison was "frantic." She filed a formal complaint alleging sexual harassment on January 30, 1987 with the IRS. She also obtained permission to transfer to San Francisco temporarily when Gray returned.

Gray sought joint counseling. He wrote Ellison another letter which still sought to maintain the idea that he and Ellison had some type of relationship.

The IRS employee investigating the allegation agreed with Ellison's supervisor that Gray's conduct constituted sexual harassment. In its final decision, however, the Treasury Department rejected Ellison's complaint because it believed that the complaint did not describe a pattern or practice of sexual harassment covered by the EEOC regulations. After an appeal, the EEOC affirmed the Treasury Department's decision on a different ground. It concluded that the agency took adequate action to prevent the repetition of Gray's conduct.

The lawsuit:

Ellison filed a complaint in September of 1987 in federal district court. The district court held that Ellison did not state a prima facie case of hostile environment sexual harassment. The appellate court disagreed and reversed the decision.

The issue:

This case introduces involves an important issue relating to the law of sexual harassment: what test should be applied to determine whether conduct is sufficiently severe or pervasive to alter the conditions of employment and create a hostile working environment?

The applicable law:

Title VII of the Civil Rights Act of 1964 makes it "an unlawful employment practice for an employer . . . to discriminate against any individual with respect to his compensation, terms, conditions, or privileges of employment, because of such individual's race, color, religion, sex, or national origin." Congress added the word "sex" to at the last minute on the floor of the House of Representatives. Virtually no legislative history provides guidance to courts interpreting the prohibition of sex discrimination. In Meritor Savings Bank v. Vinson, 477 U.S. 57, 91 L. Ed. 2d 49, 106 S. Ct. 2399 (1986), the Supreme Court held that sexual harassment constitutes sex discrimination in violation of Title VII.

Courts have recognized different forms of sexual harassment. In "quid pro quo" cases, employers condition employment benefits on sexual favors. In "hostile environment" cases, employees work in offensive or abusive environments. This case, like *Meritor*, involved a hostile environment claim.

The Supreme Court in *Meritor* held that Mechelle Vinson's working conditions constituted a hostile environment in violation of TitleVII's prohibition of sex discrimination. Vinson's supervisor made repeated demands for sexual favors, usually at work, both during and after business hours. Vinson initially refused her employer's sexual advances, but eventually acceded because she feared losing her job. They had intercourse over forty times. She additionally testified that he "fondled her in front of other employees, followed her into the women's restroom when she went there alone, exposed himself to her, and even forcibly raped her on several occasions." Meritor, 477 U.S. at 60. The Court had no difficulty finding this environment hostile. Id. at 67.

The law holds that a hostile environment exists when an employee can show (1) that he or she was subjected to sexual advances, requests for sexual favors, or other verbal or physical conduct of a sexual nature, (2) that this conduct was unwelcome, and (3) that the conduct was sufficiently severe or pervasive to alter the conditions of the victim's employment and create an abusive working environment.

Analysis and reasoning:

The Supreme Court in Meritor explained that courts may properly look to guidelines issued by the Equal Employment Opportunity Commission (EEOC) for guidance when examining hostile environment claims of sexual harassment. 477 U.S. at 65. The EEOC guidelines describe hostile environment harassment as "conduct [which] has the purpose or effect of unreasonably interfering with an individual's work performance or creating an intimidating, hostile, or offensive working environment." 29 C.F.R. § 1604.11(a)(3).

The EEOC, in accord with a substantial body of judicial decisions, has concluded, "Title VII affords employees the right to work in an environment free from discriminatory intimidation, ridicule, and insult." 477 U.S. at 65.

The Supreme Court cautioned, however, that not all harassment affects a "term, condition, or privilege" of employment within the meaning of Title VII. For example, the "mere utterance of an ethnic or racial epithet which engenders offensive feelings in an employee" is not, by itself, actionable under Title VII. Id. at 67. To state a claim under Title VII, sexual harassment "must be sufficiently severe or pervasive to alter the conditions of the victim's employment and create an abusive working environment." Id.

The Court's decision

The Ellison court found that Gray's conduct was sufficiently severe and pervasive to alter the conditions of Ellison's employment and created an abusive working environment.

The Ellison court made this decision by changing the focus of the test. Traditionally, the court evaluated by the severity of unwelcome conduct by evaluating what a reasonable person would think. In other words, what would a reasonable person in the same or similar position believe?

The Ellison court believed that this test was ineffective. In evaluating the severity and pervasiveness of sexual harassment, the court noted that it should instead focus on the perspective of the victim. Courts "should consider the victim's perspective and not stereotyped notions of acceptable behavior." If the court only examined whether a reasonable person would engage in allegedly harassing conduct, the court would run the risk of reinforcing the prevailing level of discrimination. Harassers could continue to harass merely because a particular discriminatory practice was common, and victims of harassment would have no remedy.

It is preferable to analyze harassment from the victim's perspective. A complete understanding of the victim's view requires, among other things, an analysis of the different perspectives of men and women. Conduct that many men consider unobjectionable may offend many women. See, e.g., Lipsett v. University of Puerto Rico, 864 F.2d 881, 898 (1st Cir. 1988)("A male supervisor might believe, for example, that it is legitimate for him to tell a female subordinate that she has a 'great figure' or 'nice legs.' The female subordinate, however, may find such comments offensive"); Yates, 819 F.2d at 637, n.2 ("men and women are vulnerable in different ways and offended by different behavior"). See also Ehrenreich, Pluralist Myths and Powerless Men: The Ideology of Reasonableness in Sexual Harassment Law, 99 Yale L. J. 1177, 1207-1208 (1990)(men tend to view some forms of sexual harassment as "harmless social interactions to which only overly-sensitive women would object"); Abrams, Gender Discrimination and the Transformation of Workplace Norms, 42 Vand. L. Rev. 1183, 1203 (1989) (the characteristically male view depicts sexual harassment as comparatively harmless amusement).

The court recognized that that there is a broad range of viewpoints among women as a group, but also believed that many women share common concerns which men do not necessarily share. For example, because women are disproportionately victims of rape and sexual assault, women have a stronger incentive to be concerned with sexual behavior. Women who are victims of mild forms of sexual harassment may understandably worry whether a harasser's conduct is merely a prelude to violent sexual assault. Men, who are rarely victims of sexual assault, may view sexual conduct in a vacuum without a full appreciation of the social setting or the underlying threat of violence that a woman may perceive.

In order to shield employers from having to accommodate the idiosyncratic concerns of the rare hyper-sensitive employee, we hold that a female plaintiff states a prima facie case of hostile environment sexual harassment when she alleges conduct which a reasonable woman would consider sufficiently severe or pervasive to alter the conditions of employment and create an abusive working environment.

The court adopted the perspective of a reasonable woman primarily because we believe that a sex-blind reasonable person standard tends to be male-biased and tends to systematically ignore the experiences of women. The reasonable woman standard does not establish a higher level of protection for women than men. Cf. Rosenfeld v. Southern Pacific Co., 444 F.2d 1219, 1225-1227 (9th Cir. 1971) (invalidating under Title VII paternalistic state labor laws restricting employment opportunities for women). Instead, a gender-conscious examination of sexual harassment enables women to participate in the workplace on an equal footing with men. By acknowledging and not trivializing the effects of sexual harassment on reasonable women, courts can work towards ensuring that neither men nor women will have to "run a gauntlet of sexual abuse in return for the privilege of being allowed to work and make a living." Henson v. Dundee, 682 F.2d 897, 902 (11th Cir. 1982).

The court noted that the reasonable victim standard classifies conduct as unlawful sexual harassment even when harassers do not realize that their conduct creates a hostile working environment. Well-intentioned compliments by co-workers or supervisors can form the basis of a sexual harassment cause of action if a reasonable victim of the same sex as the plaintiff would consider the comments sufficiently severe or pervasive to alter a condition of employment and create an abusive working environment. That is because Title VII is not a fault-based tort scheme. "Title VII is aimed at the consequences or effects of an employment practice and not at the . . . motivation" of co-workers or employers. Rogers, 454 F.2d at 239; see also Griggs v. Duke Power Co., 401 U.S. 424, 432, 28 L. Ed. 2d 158, 91 S. Ct. 849 (1971)(the absence of discriminatory intent does not redeem an otherwise unlawful employment practice). To avoid liability under Title VII, employers may have to educate and sensitize their workforce to eliminate conduct which a reasonable victim would consider unlawful sexual harassment. See 29 C.F.R. § 1604.11(f) ("Prevention is the best tool for the elimination of sexual harassment.")

The court noted that the facts of this case illustrate the importance of considering the victim's perspective. Analyzing the facts from the alleged harasser's viewpoint, Gray could be portrayed as a modern-day Cyrano de Bergerac wishing no more than to woo Ellison with his words. There is no evidence that Gray harbored ill will toward Ellison. He even offered in his "love letter" to leave her alone if she wished. Examined in this light, it is not difficult to see why the district court characterized Gray's conduct as isolated and trivial.

Ellison, however, did not consider the acts to be trivial. Gray's first note shocked and frightened her. After receiving the three-page letter, she became really upset and frightened again. She immediately requested that she or Gray be transferred. Her supervisor's prompt response suggests that she too did not consider the conduct trivial. When Ellison learned that Gray arranged to return to San Mateo, she immediately asked to transfer, and she immediately filed an official complaint.

The court noted that it could not say as a matter of law that Ellison's reaction was idiosyncratic or hyper-sensitive. We believe that a reasonable woman could have had a similar reaction. After receiving the first bizarre note from Gray, a person she barely knew, Ellison asked a co-worker to tell Gray to leave her alone. Despite her request, Gray sent her a long, passionate, disturbing letter. He told her he had been "watching" and "experiencing" her; he made repeated references to sex; he said he would write again. Ellison had no way of knowing what Gray would do next. A reasonable woman could consider Gray's conduct, as alleged by Ellison, sufficiently severe and pervasive to alter a condition of employment and create an abusive working environment.

Conclusion

Sexual harassment is a major problem in the workplace. Adopting the victim's perspective ensures that courts will not "sustain ingrained notions of reasonable behavior fashioned by the offenders." Lipsett, 864 F.2d at 898. Congress did not enact Title VII to codify prevailing sexist prejudices. To the contrary, "Congress designed Title VII to prevent the perpetuation of stereotypes and a sense of degradation which serve to close or discourage employment opportunities for women." Andrews, 895 F.2d at 1483. We hope that over time both men and women will learn what conduct offends reasonable members of the other sex. When employers and employees internalize the standard of workplace conduct established in this case, the current gap in perception between the sexes will be bridged.

Case note: BDO Seidman v. Hirshberg

Editor: Griffin Pivateau
Case name: BDO Seidman v. Hirshberg
Case citation: 712 N.E.2d 1220 (1999)

Introduction:

Employers are often concerned about employees leaving and taking clients or customers with them to their new employer. The law generally permits employers to restrict some of the activities of former employees. Such restrictions must, however, be supported by a legitimate business interest. It is not enough that the former employer wants to punish the employee. Legitimate business interests usually involve the preservation of confidential information and protecting the goodwill of the employer.

This case concerns a dispute between an accountant, Jeffrey Hirshberg, and his former employer, an accounting firm, BDO Seidman. BDO is a national accounting firm with 40 offices throughout the United States, including four in New York State.

Two years after Hirshberg resigned from BDO, the firm brought an action for reimbursement pursuant to the manager's agreement. BDO claimed that more than 100 former clients of its Buffalo office had been lost to Hirshberg after he had left the firm. Hirshberg denied many of the allegations. Hirshberg argued that many of the clients allegedly lost by BDO were personal clients he had brought to the firm through his own outside contacts. As for other claimed lost clients, Hirshberg maintained that he had not been the primary representative servicing the clients when they were with the firm.

Facts:

Hirshberg began working in BDO's Buffalo office in 1984, when the accounting firm he had been working for was merged into BDO. In 1989, Hirshberg was promoted to the position of manager, apparently a step immediately below attaining partner status. As a condition of receiving the promotion, Hirshberg was required to sign a "Manager's Agreement." In this agreement, Hirshberg agreed that if he served any former client of the firm's Buffalo office within 18 months following the termination of his employment, he would compensate the firm for loss and damages. The parties agreed that the damages would be calculated according to a formula contained in the agreement.

The terms of the agreement expressly acknowledged that a fiduciary relationship existed between him and the firm because he received various disclosures that would give him an advantage in attracting BDO clients. Based upon that stated premise, Hirshberg agreed that if, within 18 months following the termination of his employment, he served any former client of BDO's Buffalo office, he would compensate BDO "for the loss and damages suffered" in an amount equal to 1 1/2 times the fees BDO had charged that client over the last fiscal year of the client's patronage. Hirshberg was to pay such amount in five annual installments.

The Manager's Agreement did not prevent Hirshberg from competing for new clients, nor did it expressly bar him from serving former BDO clients. Instead, it required him to pay "for the loss and damages" sustained by BDO in losing any of its clients to Hirshberg within 18 months after his departure, an amount equivalent to 1 1/2 times the last annual billing for any such client who became the client of Hirshberg.

Hirshberg resigned from BDO in October 1993. During pretrial discovery, BDO submitted a list of 100 former clients of its Buffalo office that were lost to Hirshberg. The clients were billed a total of $ 138,000 in the year Hirshberg left the firm's practice.

BDO did not submit any evidence that Hirshberg actually solicited former clients, and did not rely in any way on claims that Hirshberg used confidential information in acquiring BDO clients.

Issue:

Did the Manager's Agreement serve a legitimate business interest of BDO?

Analysis:

The legal status of the manager's agreement

The first question that the court faced was whether the Manager's Agreement was a noncompete agreement, as that term is commonly understood. The agreement did not prevent Hirshberg from competing for new clients, nor did it expressly bar him from serving the firm's clients. Instead, the agreement required him to pay for the loss and damages sustained by the firm in losing any of its clients to Hirshberg within 18 months after his departure.

The Court found that the agreement, in its purpose and effect, was a form of employee anti-competitive agreement. Courts carefully scrutinize such agreements. Nevertheless, a no-compete agreement should be enforced to the extent that it is reasonable in time and area. This determination is determined by whether it is necessary to protect the employer's legitimate interests, not harmful to the general public, and did not unduly burden the employee.

The three-pronged test for determining the reasonableness of employee agreements not to compete

Reported cases adjudicating the validity of post-employment restrictive covenants go back almost 300 years. In the 19th century, a standard of reasonableness for judging the validity of such agreements developed in case law, both in the United States and in

England. This standard balances the need of fair protection for the benefit of the employer against the opposing interests of the former employee and the public

The modern, prevailing common-law standard of reasonableness for employee agreements not to compete applies a three-pronged test. A restraint is reasonable only if it: (1) is no greater than is required for the protection of the legitimate interest of the employer, (2) does not impose undue hardship on the employee, and (3) is not injurious to the public. A violation of any prong renders the covenant invalid.

New York adopted this prevailing standard of reasonableness in determining the validity of employee agreements not to compete. "In this context a restrictive covenant will only be subject to specific enforcement to the extent that it is reasonable in time and area, necessary to protect the employer's legitimate interests, not harmful to the general public and not unreasonably burdensome to the employee."

The court relied on the modern common-law standard of reasonableness for noncompete agreements. This three-pronged test states that the restraint was reasonable only if it: (1) was no greater than was required for the protection of the legitimate interest of the employer, (2) did not impose undue hardship on the employee, and (3) was not injurious to the public.

The parties' arguments

BDO contended that it had a legitimate interest in protecting its entire client base from competition from previous employees. It contended that the Manager's Agreement served this legitimate interest.

Hirshberg denied serving some of the clients allegedly taken from BDO. He stated further that a substantial number of the clients allegedly taken from BDO were in fact personal clients he had brought to the firm through his own outside contacts.

The court rejected BDO's arguments and sided with Hirshberg. The court found that if an employee abstained from using unfair means in competing for clients, the employer's interests in preserving its client base against the competition of the former employee was no more legitimate and worthy of contractual protection than when it vied with unrelated competitors for those clients. In other words, Hirshberg was to be treated by the courts in the same manner as any other competitor. As long as he did not use unfair means to attract former clients, BDO could not restrict Hirshberg any more than it could other competitors. His status as a former employee did not prevent him from soliciting clients once he left BDO's employ.

The employer's legitimate business interest

The court noted, however, that an employer had a legitimate interest in protecting customer relationships that an employee acquired in the course of employment. The result would be different if the accountant used confidential firm information to attract clients of the firm with whom he had not had a relationship while employed there. In that situation, the employee shared in the goodwill of a client or customer that the employer's overall efforts and expenditures created. The employer would had a legitimate interest in preventing former employees from exploiting or appropriating the goodwill of a client or customer, which had been created and maintained at the employer's expense to the employer's competitive detriment.

The court found that BDO would have a legitimate interest in protection against in an accountant's competitive use of client relationships. The firm had enabled him to acquire through his performance of accounting services for the firm's clientele during the course of his employment.

Nevertheless, extending the anti-competitive covenant to the firm's clients with whom a relationship with the accountant did not develop through assignments to perform direct, substantive accounting services would, therefore, violate the first prong of the common-law rule: it would constitute a restraint greater than was needed to protect these legitimate interests.

Conclusion

The Court concluded that the Manager's Agreement was invalid and unenforceable. It was not reasonable because it did not serve a legitimate business interest. he covenant not to compete required the accountant to compensate the firm for lost patronage of clients with whom he never had a relationship while employed at BDO. The noncompete was unreasonable in that it prohibited the accountant from providing services to his personal clients who came to BDO solely to avail themselves of his services and only as a result of his own independent recruitment efforts. The firm neither subsidized nor otherwise financially supported these clients; thus, the goodwill of those clients was not acquired through the expenditure of the firm's resources. Therefore, the firm had no legitimate interest in preventing the accountant from competing for their patronage.

Except for the overbroad restrictions, the other provisions in the agreement did not violate the rest of the three part common-law test for reasonableness. The restraint was limited to a reasonable time and to a reasonable geographic area. The accountant was free to compete immediately for new business in any market and, if the overbroad provisions of the covenant were struck, to retain his personal clients and those clients of firm's that he had not served to any significant extent while employed at the firm.

Article: Restraints on employee mobility

Introduction

In the last decade, the business environment changed. Companies today face numerous challenges: worldwide competitors, changes in information technology, increased reliance on trained workers, and a shifting economic environment. In response to these new pressures, organizations have adopted new processes, modified internal structures, and embraced a number of other changes.

Competitive pressures have led managers to focus on their employees as drivers of productivity. Employees are, in a sense, a collective asset of an organization. Employees make up the human capital of the company. Although intangible, human capital is just as real, and just as important, as physical assets.

Traditionally, companies have sought competitive advantage by reducing costs and introducing new products. But companies have learned that continual cost cutting is not a long term solution. Competing on cost alone is difficult. As industries become increasingly commoditized, lower costs are available to most competitors and are easily matched. Similarly, even a constant supply of innovative products cannot guarantee a competitive advantage. In fast-moving, high-technology industries, for example, a company can relentlessly produce new products and still struggle to keep up with competitors.

Therefore, companies should seek to maximize their human capital. Logically, an organization that invests in its human capital will be rewarded with increased productivity and higher returns. But there is a problem with this reasoning. Although it may make theoretical sense to label human capital as an asset, employees differ from other forms of assets. An organization cannot have an ownership interest in its employees and the human capital that they represent. Instead, only the employment relationship secures the retention of human capital.

Investment in employees can lead to a paradox. A company that invests in its employees, providing those employees with new skills and knowledge, has increased the employee's value. This added value may or may not correspond to increased value for the employer. Instead, these gained skills, knowledge, and experience will enhance the employee's marketability, permitting her to transfer the benefits of the organization's investment to a competitor. A company that invests in human capital without taking steps to secure that capital may discover its investment flowing to the competition.

An employer will invest in human capital to increase performance, to reduce costs, and to improve efficiency. An employer who invests in human capital can expect to reap rewards in the form of increased productivity and profit. Investments in training people and developing talent provide a way of attracting and retaining employees. Human capital theory proposes that organizations' investments in people will lead to returns that exceed those investments.

The employee can also expect to benefit from the organization's investment in human capital. The employee will often receive greater income, higher satisfaction from the performance of her duties, opportunities for advancement, and perhaps greater job security. Unfortunately for the organization, its investment in the employee will also likely permit the employee to receive training, experience, and a skill set that will further enhance the employee's marketability. An investment in human capital may increase the employee's value, while also enhancing the likelihood that the employee will transfer those skills to another organization.

Employment law provides several tools to retain employees. The best tool to address the problem of preservation and retention of the organization's human capital is the noncompete agreement. A noncompete agreement, carefully drafted and tailored to the employee's situation, will help firms retain the benefits of investment in their workforce. Employees who are governed by a noncompete agreement are less likely to leave the company. In the event that an employee decides to leave, the noncompete agreement will prevent this employee from immediately taking her new skills and experience to a competitor.

This chapter discusses the drafting of an enforceable noncompete agreement. To ensure the validity of the agreements, organizations must be careful in drafting. Historically, courts have historically with disfavor on noncompete agreements. As a result, there is always the potential that a court may choose not to enforce the agreement. Moreover, there are differences in the way that states interpret the noncompete agreements. Therefore, effective drafting of noncompete agreements is vital.

Use of the Noncompete Agreement as a Management Tool

Understanding the noncompete agreement

A noncompete agreement is an agreement in which the employee agrees for a specific period of time and within a particular area to refrain from competition with his employer. The noncompete agreement is known by other names, most notably as a "covenant not-to-compete," a "restrictive covenant," or a "non-compete clause." These terms are interchangeable and all refer to an employment contract or provision purporting to limit an employee's power upon leaving his or her employment, to compete in the market in which the former employer does business.

In the employment context, noncompete agreements are generally directed at four discrete areas: (1) general noncompetition; (2) customer (or client) non-solicitation; (3) employee non-solicitation; and (4) non-disclosure. But these four different areas are regularly intermingled. Noncompete agreements may, and often do, contain some or all of these protective clauses.

Noncompete agreements, in theory at least, are not meant to punish the former employee. Instead, they are meant to protect the employer from unfair competition. Noncompete agreements arguably protect an employer's customer base, trade secrets, and other information vital to its success. From this perspective, noncompete agreements encourage employers to invest in their employees. An employer does not wish to invest in an employee only to see the employee take the skills acquired, or the company's customers, to another employer. Logically, the employer will invest more in the employee if measures are in place to guard against the employee's movement to a competitor.

A carefully crafted noncompete agreement will prevent employers from losing employees

The noncompete agreement discourages employee movement. An enforceable noncompete agreement will prevent an employee from working for a competitor for a specified length of time. Arguably, there are few employees that can readily absorb a long term of inactivity, a term that could last up to three years based on a typical noncompete agreement. While noncompete agreements do not completely cure employee turnover, they act as a considerable deterrent. A noncompete agreement, even if never enforced, will provide a strong disincentive to leave a job.

Moreover, an employee restrained by a noncompete agreement will have a more difficult time finding a new place to work. Employers understand that it is difficult to poach employees who have agreed to a noncompete agreement. An organization seeking to hire away key employees from a competitor will be aware that those employees may not be able to start work in the near term. An employee forced to the sidelines for a year or more is considerably less desirable to another employer.

The noncompete agreement inhibits competitors in another way. A company that hires an employee away from a competitor, knowing that the employee has a contractual obligation to not work for a competitor, runs the risk of being sued for tortious interference with a contract. A company that encourages a new hire to breach her noncompete agreement may be liable for sued for this tort. Thus, the original employer may have a suit not only against its former employee for breach of the noncompete agreement, but also against the hiring competitor for encouraging the former employee to breach her contractual obligations. This is a powerful weapon for employers.

Crafting an Enforceable Noncompete Agreement

Noncompete agreements must be reasonable

Courts have traditionally viewed noncompete agreements with disfavor, believing that the agreements contravene public policy. Because the agreements were seen as unfair restraints on trade, the common law prohibited the use of such agreements. Courts routinely refused to enforce noncompete agreements. In time, the restrictions on such agreements lessened. Nevertheless, the common law has generally restricted their use for any purpose other than for legitimate business purposes. To ensure the purpose is legitimate, the law requires that a valid noncompete agreement meet a reasonableness requirement.

The reasonableness requirement is designed to balance the interests of all entities affected by the noncompete agreement: the employer, the employee, and society as a whole. Each entity has an interest to be protected. The employee wishes to preserve his mobility; the employer wishes to protect itself from unfair competition; and society wishes to balance with a system that provides incentives for the development and training of employees. With so many varied interests at hand, the successfully drafted noncompete agreement must be drafted carefully as to satisfy all three stakeholders.

To satisfy the reasonableness requirement, the law requires that the employer establish a reason for the noncompete agreement other than preventing the employee from competing with his former employer. There must be some element to the competition that would make such competition unfair. The employer's justification cannot simply consist of the training or experience gained while on the job because an employee has a right to those things. Instead, the employer must demonstrate the existence of "special circumstances" that are present to justify the use of the noncompete agreement.

Courts have acknowledged two goals as sufficient justification for the execution of a noncompete agreement. An employer is entitled to (1) protect the goodwill of its business, and (2) protect its trade secrets.

An employee often generates goodwill in his conduct with clients, fostering personal relationships with customers. That goodwill does not, however, belong to the employee, who has conducted business as an agent of the employer. Instead, the goodwill is an asset of the employer. The law protects these corporate customer relations as part of the "customer contact" theory.

The employer also has a right to protect its trade secrets. An employer can utilize a number of legal documents to secure these secrets. Still, a noncompete agreement is useful as a supplementary form of protection. The noncompete agreement protects trade secrets in the best manner possible—by preventing the former employee from working for a competitor. Thus, the employer is able to prevent the sharing of trade secrets before the disclosure ever takes place. A noncompete agreement is a strong prophylactic remedy that aims to prevent unwanted disclosures rather than having to sue for misappropriation of trade secrets after the fact.

Enforcement of the Noncompete Agreement Requires a Carefully Drafted Document

Establishing the existence of a legitimate business interest to be protected is merely the threshold step that an employer must meet to create an enforceable agreement. The scope of the noncompete agreement must not be greater than the business interest at stake. Almost all courts apply a standard of reasonableness in deciding whether to enforce a noncompete agreement. As will be seen below, however, "reasonableness" as a standard holds minimal value in the construction of noncompete agreements.

Nineteen states provide a statutory framework for the regulation of noncompete agreements. In contrast, the remaining states rely on the court system. In common law jurisdictions, a noncompete agreement will be upheld only "if the restraint imposed is not unreasonable, is founded on a valuable consideration, and is reasonably necessary to protect the interest of the party in whose favor it is imposed, and does not unduly prejudice the interests of the public."

Many states follow the test set forth in the Restatement (Second) of Contracts, which takes into consideration the following factors:

(1) whether the restriction is greater than necessary to protect the business and goodwill of the employer;

(2) whether the employer's need for protection outweighs the economic hardship which the covenant imposes on the departing party; and

(3) whether the restriction adversely affects the interests of the public.

Once a court determines that the noncompete agreement protects a legitimate business interest, it will then examine the agreement to ensure that it does not exceed the minimum restraint necessary to protect that interest. Courts will enforce agreements only where they are "strictly limited in time and territorial effect and . . . [are] otherwise reasonable considering the business interest of the employer sought to be protected and the effect on the employee." In common law jurisdictions, noncompete agreements are enforced as reasonable if they are found to satisfy the following three elements:

Thus, to be enforceable, agreements must be reasonable in three ways: scope (referring to the subject matter of the agreement), duration, and geography.

Limitations on Scope of Activity

There are two general types of scope of activity limitations: those that prohibit the employee from soliciting the employer's customers and those that prohibit the employee from engaging in any competitive business. With respect to customer solicitation, reasonable limitations are valid and enforceable. A legitimate purpose of a noncompete agreement is to prevent employees or departing partners from using the business contacts and rapport established while representing a firm to take the firm's customers with him." As an example, noncompete agreements that are limited to those customers with whom the employee had regular contact on a personal level would likely be deemed reasonable.

Limitations on Time

The duration of the restriction is a factor used by courts to determine reasonableness. Restraints that are unlimited in time are almost always unreasonable. However, it is necessary to consider the particular industry at issue to determine whether the particular restraint is reasonable as to time. The courts' inconsistent analysis under this fact-specific inquiry is frustrating.

A look at the cases finds courts upholding restrictive covenants that last as long as five or ten years, while invalidating others that last only one or two years. Moreover, courts in the same jurisdiction will uphold a three-year limitation in one case but invalidate it in another. Unfortunately, in so doing the courts seldom attempt to reconcile their decisions, except perhaps by concluding that each case must be decided on its own facts. In reviewing the cases, it appears almost as if courts decide cases on a whim. This failure to provide a bright-line rule makes it difficult for those drafting noncompete agreements.

A review of case law indicates that most courts usually uphold time limitations of one or two years. While limitations of three to five years may be upheld in the sale of a business, the decisions conflict as to whether a three to five year limitation is reasonable in an employment situation.

Limitations on Geography

The geographical limitation in a noncompete agreement must be definite. An indefinite description of the geographical area should render the agreement unenforceable as written. What is a permissible geographic restriction?

Traditionally, the reasonableness of a geographic limitation was directly related to the location of the territory in which the employee worked for his former employer. Courts have found that geographic restraints were reasonable if the area of the restraint is no broader than the territory throughout which the employee was able to establish contact with his employer's customers during the term of his employment.

Numerous courts have found that a reasonable area consists of the territory in which the employee worked while employed. Beyond this general rule, however, what constitutes a reasonable geographical area invariably depends upon the facts of the specific case.

The Effect of the Blue-Pencil Doctrine

Traditionally, under the common law, courts rarely enforced unreasonable agreements in part. An agreement made unreasonable by attempting to overextend its prohibitions would be either invalidated completely, or the offending passage could be deleted pursuant to the blue-pencil doctrine. The blue-pencil test is a judicial standard by which courts may invalidate the whole contract or only the offending words of the contract. If the blue-pencil doctrine is strictly applied, only the offending words are invalidated if it would be possible to delete them simply by running a blue-pencil through them, as opposed to changing, adding, or rearranging words. The blue-pencil doctrine is based in large part on the understanding that there is not necessarily a sinister purpose behind an overly broad noncompete. In other words, an employer may unintentionally use language beyond that which would be considered reasonable. Courts can and do look to the good faith of the employer in determining whether to utilize the blue-pencil doctrine.

Application of the blue pencil doctrine depends on state law. A court may do one of three things. In the most severe application of the blue pencil doctrine, in "all or nothing" states, a court will void the entire noncompete agreement if any clause is unenforceable.

The second approach is known as the strict blue-pencil rule. The strict blue-pencil rule does not allow courts to rewrite overbroad noncompete agreements. Instead, the strict approach allows courts only to strike overbroad provisions and enforce what is left of the agreement. Enforcement is permitted only if the agreement is reasonably limited after the overbroad provisions have been removed.

Finally, other states have adopted a liberal form of the blue-pencil doctrine: the "reasonable modification" approach. These states permit a court to rewrite an overbroad non-competition agreement to reasonably limit the restrictions found in the agreement.

How to Draft a Noncompete Agreement

A noncompete agreement can be drafted so that a court will enforce it
The best thing that a drafter can do to ensure enforcement is to individualize the agreement as much as possible. The closer aligned the agreement is with the actual nature of the employee's position, the more likely it is to be enforced.

The law will only support a noncompete agreement that is based on legitimate purposes. As discussed above, those purposes are generally are based on employer goodwill and trade secrets. Thus, the employer should begin by looking at the employee and determining whether this employee, and this position, should be restrained. In short, an employer must ask whether a legitimate purpose is being served with a particular noncompete agreement. To ensure a greater chance of enforcement, it may be worthwhile to explicitly name the purpose being served.

Once the employer has committed to the noncompete agreement, it is best to determine how the agreement will be constrained. As noted, a noncompete agreement must be constrained in three ways: by scope of activity, by geography, and by time.

The contractual clause limiting the scope of the employee's activity must relate to the work that the employee is actually doing, not what the employee was hired to do or what the employee could do in the future. Because a noncompete agreement must serve a legitimate purpose, the scope of activity that the employer is seeking to restrain must be related to one of the purposes discussed above: either goodwill or trade secrets. The noncompete agreement cannot function as a restraint only for restraint purposes—instead it is restraint to prevent unfair competition. Thus, when drafting a noncompete agreement, the employer should review the employee's job duties. The noncompete agreement should reflect a restraint on similar duties. A noncompete agreement that stretches too far in the type of work that it seeks to limit invites a challenge.

The noncompete agreement must be limited by time. The time period will differ depending on the interest that the noncompete agreement is protecting. If a worker in a technical field is bound by a noncompete agreement, it is much more likely that a court will view the time limit with suspicion. Because technology changes rapidly, an agreement that seeks to restrain an employee for a long period of time will be hard-pressed to stand up in court. If the legitimate interest being served is protection against unfair competition, a court is likely to find that binding an employee for a lengthy time does not serve that interest because technology changes quickly.

When deciding on an appropriate time restriction, employers should carefully review the work that the employee is doing to ensure that the time limit matches the job responsibilities. Lower-level employees may be able to challenge a lengthy time restriction, while a longer time restriction would likely prove valid for upper-level employees.

Still, how long can one restrict an employee? The answer, unfortunately, is not clear. Traditionally, courts upheld restrictions for less than two years, while viewing anything more than that very carefully. Although there has never been a uniformly-enforced time period, the recent trend is for courts to enforce longer time limits. Recent cases have seen support for time limits over two years. For those employers in blue-pencil states, it is worthwhile to err on the upper side of a time limit, since employers can be confident that a court interested in reformation of the agreement will simply amend the time restriction. A court need not look very hard at time limit to lower it.

Drafting a Noncompete Agreement that a Court Will Enforce

It is possible to create an agreement that is more likely to be enforced. In every state that enforces noncompete agreements, the threshold inquiry is one of reasonableness. This reasonableness requirement is in place to ensure that the noncompete agreement extends no further than to protect the legitimate business interest that is served by the noncompete. Having determined that such a business interest is served, the court will next conduct a reasonableness inquiry.

The reasonableness inquiry consists of an independent analysis of three separate elements: the scope of the activity to be restricted, the geographic location in which the activity is to be restricted, and the time for which the activity is to be restricted.

Calculating the Time Restraint

Although rarely acknowledged expressly, it is the time element that a court will examine first. Such placement in the chain of analysis is logical. An examination of the time requirement can be made quickly, requiring very little work on behalf of the court. A review of case law reveals that certain bounds are essentially predetermined, no matter what the scope or geography limitation. A time period of five years is unlikely to be upheld, but a court will likely view a time period of a year or less as reasonable.

From a strategic viewpoint, consider the value of the particular employee, the importance of the position to the company, and the reason why this employee's work for a competitor would either provide an unfair advantage to a competitor or damage the goodwill of the company. An employer should seek to restrain an employee only to the extent outlined, or risk having the agreement fail completely or reformed by the court.

Calculating the Scope of Activity Restraint

Having made a decision as to the time in which the employee is to be restrained, the employer should look at what activities are to be restrained. Remember that the purpose of the noncompete is to prevent unfair competition. For that reason, the scope of the activity to be restrained should resemble the scope of the employee's current position. An employer can determine this first by looking at the job description for the employee's current position. This job description should accurately describe what it is that the employee does. The proposed noncompete agreement should describe with some particularity the activities the employee is restrained from performing. The key is specificity; a court is more likely to enforce an agreement if it can readily determine that the provisions are not mere boilerplate.

The scope of activity limitation raises another issue. A noncompete agreement should be updated if the employee's position or responsibilities change. It is not uncommon for an employee's responsibilities to grow over time; often an employee will begin work for a firm and then be promoted within the organization. At the time of the employee's separation from the organization, the job responsibilities may far exceed those that existed when the employee started. An employer should expect that an employee's noncompete agreement will change during the course of his career.

This need to modify an agreement over time should not pose a significant burden on the employer. One can presume that as new pay and benefit packages are prepared, an opportune time to revisit the noncompete agreement arises. It is also advisable to discuss, at the time of signing, that execution of a revised noncompete agreement is a normal part of the company's employee retention scheme. Assumedly, an employee is less likely to balk at the noncompete agreement when it is presented in conjunction with a promotion, increased salary, or other similar items.

Drafting the Geographic Restraint

Having conquered the first two hurdles, only the question of the noncompete agreement's geographic restraint remains. This restraint, once so easily understood by courts, employers, and employees, has also grown much more problematic in recent years. The geographic limitation was originally aimed at preventing unfair competition in the area in which the employer did business. In recent years, the geographic ranges of businesses have expanded tremendously. Organizations that at one time might have limited themselves to a customer base living within ten square miles of the business are now doing business throughout the state, across the nation, and worldwide. Salesmen who might once have limited themselves to a three county area are now able to peddle their goods to customers regardless of their location.

This growth in geographic sales range is not merely the result of the internet. Barriers to commerce have increasingly shrunk, with the advent of inexpensive telephone service, and other technological advances. In any event, one can easily suppose that the business range of most companies has expanded greatly within the last decade.

Despite these advances, employers have benefitted from the opinion of some courts that geographic location need not be enforced quite as strongly as the other requirements. Nationwide bans have been upheld. Sometimes, even worldwide restrictions have been considered valid.

What then should we make of the geographic component of the noncompete agreement? As a result of these decisions, to what extent should an employer attempt to restrain the geographic range of its ex-employees? The starting point should again be the nature of the employee's current position. In what geographic region does the employee currently work? What is the actual market for the company's products? One may argue that, because a company sells products on the web, it has a worldwide scope. However, courts will not likely accept such an argument without evidence to establish that a percentage of a company's products are actually sold worldwide.

There are alternative legal means to retain employees

Nondisclosure agreements will protect trade secrets

Some have said that noncompetition agreements are essentially a form of intellectual property regulation. Of course, employers concerned about their confidential information making its way into the hands of competitors should require employees to sign a nondisclosure agreement to protect those secrets. Unlike the severe scrutiny given to noncompetition agreements, courts will routinely intervene to prevent an employee from revealing trade secrets, confidential information, and other similar material.

Most states have adopted some form of the Uniform Trade Secret Act (the "UTSA"). The USTA provides guidelines for employers. The guiding principle of courts in determining whether to enjoin the former employee's behavior is whether the employer is protecting its legitimate business interests. The USTA provides that "actual or threatened misappropriation may be enjoined." Unfortunately, the UTSA does not define the term "threatened" misappropriation.

Inevitable disclosure doctrine

Closely related to trade secret law is the notion of 'inevitable disclosure.' Sometimes, employees can be prevented from working for a competitor, even where a noncompete agreement may not exist. Such situations often arise in the high tech world, where employees may have access to valuable proprietary information, such as intellectual property. The "inevitable disclosure" doctrine permits a court to prohibit a former employee from working for the former employer's competitor, if the employer establishes that the employee will inevitably disclose a trade secret. In determining whether to stop the employee from working for the competitor, a court will examine (a) whether the employee's knowledge is specialized and technical, (b) whether the knowledge would give the competitor a significant advantage in the market, and (c) could the employee perform his work without reference to this knowledge. If an employee could not perform his work without use or disclosure of the trade secret, then a court may intervene.

The inevitable disclosure doctrine holds that certain employees cannot "wipe clean" their knowledge of their former employers' trade secrets. Despite an employee's best efforts to avoid disclosing any trade secrets to the new employer, the employee will inevitably disclose trade secrets simply by virtue of the employment, and therefore should be enjoined from working for the new employer for some period of time, even in the absence of any non-compete agreement. Courts have justified the rule by recognizing that it is difficult for the human mind to compartmentalize and selectively suppress information, even if the employee takes great effort to do so. The doctrine of inevitable disclosure provides a possible source of relief against improper competition by former employees even where the employer cannot show actual misuse, or intent to misuse, confidential or trade secret information.

A leading case explaining the inevitable disclosure doctrine is *PepsiCo Inc. v. Redmond,* 54 F.3d 1262 (7th Cir. 1995). A marketing executive left PepsiCo, which manufactured a sports drink called "All Sport," and went to work for Quaker Oats, which manufactured "Gatorade." Redmond had knowledge of PepsiCo's strategic plans, pricing structures, attack plans for specific markets and selling and delivery systems. PepsiCo sought an injunction preventing Redmond and Quaker Oats from divulging trade secrets and confidential information. The court concluded that Redmond would inevitably disclose a trade secret, finding that "unless Redmond possessed an uncanny ability to compartmentalize information," he would necessarily be making decisions about Gatorade and Snapple by relying on PepsiCo's trade secrets. These secrets would include the "particularized plans or processes developed by [PepsiCo] and disclosed to him while the employer-employee relationship existed, which are unknown to others in the industry and which give the employer an advantage over his competitors."

The inevitable disclosure doctrine is governed by state law, so businesses should look carefully at the law in their state. For instance, California courts have rejected the inevitable disclosure doctrine, finding that it is directly contrary to California's public policy prohibiting an employer from entering into a noncompetition agreement with its employees. Courts applying California law have routinely found that the inevitable disclosure doctrine would create an after-the-fact noncompetition agreement restricting employee mobility.

Conclusion

Employees represent a valuable asset of any organization. The retention of employees should always be a management concern. The law provides several tools for retention of employees. A carefully drafted noncompete agreement can ensure that an organization, and not its competitors, will gain from investing in its employees.

About the author

Griffin Pivateau is an assistant professor of legal studies in business at the Spears School of Business at Oklahoma State University, specializing in employment law. His research interests focus on the intersection between law and business strategy, assisting business managers to achieve competitive advantage using the law. He has written extensively on matters of employee mobility and retention. His research has been cited by numerous courts and other scholars.

Before joining the faculty at Oklahoma State University, Pivateau practiced law in New Orleans, Louisiana and Houston, Texas. Pivateau graduated from the University of Texas School of Law. Prior to law school, he attended graduate school at Southern Methodist University, where he studied Spanish Colonial America under the direction of well-known scholar David J. Weber.

CPSIA information can be obtained at www.ICGtesting.com
Printed in the USA
LVOW03s1452030114

367825LV00008B/18/P